# ACTS

## THE CHURCH AT WORK

# ACTS

## THE CHURCH AT WORK

**GERALD L. STOVER**

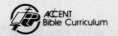

ACCENT
Bible Curriculum

**ADULT STUDENT**
Bible Study Guide

This Bible study guide is part of an adult
curriculum designed to assist you in making
the entire Bible your guide for daily living.

Gerald L. Stover/Author
Judy Stonecipher/Managing Editor
James T. Dyet/Executive Editor
Robert L. Mosier/Publisher

*Accent Bible Curriculum*
*Accent Publications, Inc.*
*12100 W. Sixth Avenue*
*P.O. Box 15337*
*Denver, Colorado 80215*

# CONTENTS

# PICTURE IT...

... a majestic cathedral set high on a hill. The windows fairly glisten in the sunlight, sending forth rainbows of color in the form of beautiful pictures. The clear, high tones of a bell ring out through the air, summoning worshipers to come and take their places. We travel up the cobblestone walkway across the lush green carpet, finally reaching the smooth pavement in front of the beautiful edifice. The spire stretches into the air many, many feet above us, seeming to touch the clouds. The marble staircase ascends into the golden interior, and we watch as hundreds of people file into the building to present their offerings and say their prayers. But is this the church?

Let us go on to another land, far away from this land of stained glass and chimes. The sky is ominous, and it looks as though it could rain. The land around is barren except for a few dead or diseased trees. The only sounds for miles are the wind and the loud cries of vultures looking for carrion to feast upon. As we walk, we feel as though we are completely isolated from the world. There is not a man in sight, and the only signs of men having ever been here are some scraps of paper rustling in the howling wind.

But suddenly, up ahead, we see a light. It looks so inviting that we instinctively turn toward it. As we near the building the light is shining from, we see people gliding silently toward the door. They stop and look all around before touching the knob, as if they are afraid of something or someone. When we finally reach the building, a man welcomes us and invites us to come in. As we stoop to enter the door, we notice that not a soul is in sight except for the man and a woman in the tiny kitchen. Then we notice it—a trapdoor in the far corner of the room. The man guides us to the door, and we descend the ladder into a musty, pitch black room. Finally the man descends with his wife, pulling the door shut over his head. A lantern jumps into flame, then another and another. The room is filled with light, and we look around us at the smiling faces. The people are dressed in rags, but their faces tell us that they do not mind the poverty or discomfort they experience. They are here for one reason—to worship their Saviour. Their voices unite in praise to the One who gave His blood for them, to redeem them from the curse of sin. Then all is hushed as an elderly man reaches into a wooden box and pulls out a tattered book. He opens it and begins reading aloud. His eyes fill with tears at the precious words flowing from his lips. And those around him also weep with joy at the message of God.

Yes, this—*this* is the church. God's people, gathered together to praise Him and to build up one another. No matter how difficult the circumstance; no matter how humble the surroundings; God's church is alive, serving Him, in all parts of the world.

The New Testament book of Acts, authored by a physician named Luke, is a history of the early church, comprised at first of thousands of Jews who had turned to Christ as their Messiah. Soon, however, the church began to grow, and the believers scattered to all parts of the globe. Persecution followed them wherever they went, but it served only to unite them and increase their ranks. The devil's servants tried countless times to destroy the church, or at least to silence its hated message, but the believers who were touched by the persecution only drew closer to the Saviour, drawing strength from Him. They also drew closer to one another, encouraging, comforting, helping, strengthening. Many believers sold every possession they owned to help less fortunate brothers. Others stood by, helpless, and watched their loved ones being tortured. Still others met with death at the stake, the dungeon. But God's church was not to be destroyed. Just as metal becomes stronger and purer when it is heated and pounded repeatedly, so the church of Jesus Christ became stronger when it met persecution.

The church has survived fierce persecutions through the centuries and is now nearly two thousand years old. But is the church as strong as it once was? Have we grown complacent, even apathetic about the lost multitudes around us? Has our prosperity made us deaf to the cries of those who are hungry for the Saviour?

We need to be once more the powerful witness for Christ that the early believers were. We need to give our all for the Lord, no matter what that may involve. He gave His life for us; the least we can do is give our lives to Him to use for His glory.

The church should be at work spreading the gospel to all parts of the globe. We should want nothing more than to glorify the Lord Jesus Christ by serving Him in whatever capacity He chooses. We need to look to the example of the first-century believers, who would stop at nothing to declare the gospel to the lost and build up one another.

The church at work will find that the Lord is faithful and will not allow us to suffer beyond what we are able to endure. He will give us strength to bear everything that comes our way, just as He did the early believers. And He will bless us abundantly, providing our every need and giving us untold spiritual blessings. This was the testimony of the first-century church, the church at work. And it can be ours, too.

# CHRIST'S COMMISSION TO BELIEVERS
### ACTS 1:1-8

## EVERY DAY WITH THE WORD

| | | |
|---|---|---|
| Monday | All power | Matthew 28 |
| Tuesday | The gospel for all | Mark 16 |
| Wednesday | Witnesses | Luke 24:36-53 |
| Thursday | Sent ones | John 20:19-31 |
| Friday | Debtors | Romans 1:1-16 |
| Saturday | Ambassadors | II Corinthians 5 |
| Sunday | Servants of the living God | I Thessalonians 1 |

Many of the early Christians found their greatest satisfaction in seeing men come to know the Saviour. This was especially true of the Apostle Paul (Romans 1:1-16).

Sir William Macgregor once discussed with a friend the rapid progress of Mohammedanism in West Africa, as compared to Christianity's slow growth.

"It's just this," he commented, "every Mohammedan regards himself as a missionary; the majority of Christians think it is another man's job."

This was not the attitude of the Christians we read about in Acts. Their unfailing zeal and their bold spirit pushed back the frontiers of paganism and darkness. Imperial Rome was rocked from east to west by the impact of the gospel. Even when the state decreed Christianity illegal, many earnest believers remained faithful. Hundreds went to their deaths, singing praise to the Lord. The gory floggings, the burnings and the wild beasts—none of these could silence the lips of the early Christians.

## PREPARATION FOR WITNESS
(Acts 1:1-5)

Luke, the author of Acts, possessed many gifts. It is clear from Scripture that he was a physician who traveled with the Apostle Paul as a medical advisor and companion. Luke was also a gifted historian, as is evident from his Gospel as well as from the book of Acts. He was a deeply loyal friend, a devoted companion in labor, and an ardent traveler.

The book of Acts, Luke's second work, has four major divisions: I. Preparation for Worldwide Witness (Acts 1); II. The Witness of the Church in Jerusalem (Acts 2—7); III. The Witness of the Church in Transition (Acts 8—12); IV. The Witness to the Regions Beyond (Acts 13—28).

The book of Acts supplies us with the first written history of the early church. And, since it is a verbally inspired document, it is fully reliable. Dated about A.D. 61, Acts covers a period of sacred history from A.D. 32 to approximately A.D. 63. This includes the two years of Paul's first imprisonment.

The believers of the first century bequeathed to the believers of the church age a rich heritage of doctrine, practice, zeal, dedication and holiness. Churches today are New Testament churches in proportion to their conformity to the apostles' doctrine and the practices of the early churches.

The beginning of the early Christians' fruitful ministry can be traced to the post-resurrection ministry of Christ. During this time the disciples received infallible proofs (Acts 1:3) that Christ was alive after His death and burial. For forty days He showed Himself to be alive. People saw

Luke was a Gentile, which is clear from the fact that Paul distinguishes him from those "of the circumcision" in Colossians 4:10-14. It is generally believed that he was a native of Antioch in Syria.

Look upon Acts as a bridge between the Gospels and the Epistles.

12

Him, heard Him speak, and ate with Him. Yes, Jesus Christ was alive! And He is alive today too!

Strangely enough, the disciples were not told to rush out immediately and spread the news that Christ was risen from the grave. Instead, the Lord commanded them to wait in Jerusalem until they were endued with power from on high (verses 4,5). The reason for this is there was much to be done before the Holy Spirit would come. The Great Commission of Acts 1:8 was to be given to the believers; Jesus was to ascend into Heaven (verses 9,10); the promise of the second coming was to be confirmed (verse 11); preparation for the appointment of one to replace Judas Iscariot was to be made (verses 15-26). The disciples didn't foresee these events; they just knew they were to wait.

Unfortunately, believers are often impatient. Sometimes older Christians become impatient with a young believer who doesn't grow spiritually as rapidly as they think he should. Frequently church leaders do not see the results they expect, so they employ methods which the Holy Spirit cannot honor. Sometimes a pastorless church rushes ahead without much prayer and calls a pastor.

But impatience has no place in the life of a Christian or a church. The early believers no doubt wondered why Christ instructed them to wait, but they were not impatient. They simply obeyed the Saviour, trusting His wisdom.

How little these early Christians knew of what lay before them—beatings, imprisonments, and even death by unbelievably cruel means. The day would come when they would need power not only for ministry but also to bear suffering for His

See Luke 24:49.

*Wait*: See Psalm 25:3; 27:14; 33:20; 37:7; 123:2; and Isaiah 40:31.

A mark of maturity is the ability to postpone a present enjoyment for the

13

name's sake. It was God's purpose to prepare them by equipping them with spiritual power. Therefore, they were to wait for the Holy Spirit's arrival.

sake of a future, greater good.

## PLAN FOR WITNESS
(Acts 1:6-8)

In the question, "Lord, wilt thou at this time restore again the kingdom to Israel?" (verse 6), the apostles were expressing their national hope. They knew it was the purpose of God to restore the kingdom to Israel in the future of Messiah's power and glory. So they reasoned, "Could it be God's purpose to do so now?"

See Isaiah 11; Jeremiah 23:3-8; Amos 9:11-15; Zechariah 14; Luke 1:32,33.

Jesus did not rebuke the disciples for their question. Nor did He destroy their confidence in a future restoration of Israel. However, He pointed out that the Father had locked up the times and seasons in His own counsel. It was not God's purpose to reveal this information to them. Instead, Christ promised: "Ye shall receive power, after that the Holy Ghost is come upon you: and ye shall be witnesses unto me both in Jerusalem, and in all Judaea, and in Samaria, and unto the uttermost part of the earth" (verse 8).

Why does the world need a witness? It is depraved (Ephesians 4:17-19); dead (Ephesians 2:1); lost (II Corinthians 4:3); blind (II Corinthians 4:4); and condemned (John 3:36; Romans 3:19,20).

There is positively no substitute for the power of the Spirit upon the ministry of a man or a church. Academic attainments, ordination certificates, diplomas for leadership training, personality—these are not, and never will be, accepted by God in exchange for His power. Only God's power can accomplish God's work.

Obedience is the pathway to power. In fact, obedience is the pathway to every blessing from God. Have you ever considered what we lose

The power of God not only gives the ability to present the truth of

God, but it also is able to bring conviction of sin and spiritual response to those who hear the Word.

through our disobedience to God? We are the ones who limit what God can do through us, for God works through us in proportion to our obedience to His Word.

The early believers experienced God's power as they testified about Jesus Christ, crucified and risen from the dead (I Corinthians 15:3,4; I Thessalonians 4:14). God's purpose is for a similar witness to be worldwide in its outreach. Churches must not merely "run a program" or "do church work." They must give a strong, aggressive, growing testimony for the Son of God.

The words "in Jerusalem, and in all Judaea, and in Samaria, and unto the uttermost part of the earth" (Acts 1:8) indicate that the program of God was to be ever expanding. The gospel was not to be hoarded by the church at Jerusalem. Of course Jerusalem was important, being the hub of Judaism. But the gospel was not to be bottled up in this city. It was to be on the move. The watchword was *progress*, and the message was to be preached to the ends of the earth. From Jerusalem it was to extend to all Judaea, to Samaria, and to the regions beyond. And it is still God's plan that His people spread His message to all parts of the globe.

Are you concerned enough about the lost to pray at the beginning of each day for the Spirit to lead you so that your witness for Christ will count to the maximum? Or do you subscribe to the belief that missions is exclusively the business of the church? Do you make the mistake of refusing to do anything to spread the gospel abroad because "we must not move out with the gospel until we completely evangelize our own society"? Have you surrendered your sons and daughters to

Someone has said: "The church must evangelize or it will fossilize."

God for service, or have you discouraged their participation in world evangelization?

Do you pray for a world without Christ? Do you personally know how to lead a soul to Christ? How much do you really care about the lost? What kind of an accounting will you give in the day when every Christian stands before the Judgment Seat of Christ? What will you say when Jesus Christ evaluates the use of your time, strength, and talents?

Romans 14:12; II Corinthians 5:10

To witness with power is an unparalleled privilege, and it should be our constant joy. Time invested in witnessing for Christ will multiply itself in redeemed souls, and thereby bring untold blessing to your life.

Psalm 126:5,6

## FOOD FOR THOUGHT

*"Do not pray for easy lives. Pray to be stronger men. Do not pray for tasks equal to your powers. Pray for powers equal to your tasks."*

—Phillips Brooks

*Answer true or false:*

1. The author of Acts was Barnabas.

2. The same person wrote Acts and the third Gospel.

3. The risen Christ showed Himself to the disciples.

4. The promise of Acts 1:4 refers to Christ's second coming.

5. The apostles believed it was God's purpose to restore the kingdom to Israel.

6. In Acts 1:7 the Lord Jesus rebuked the apostles for their interest in the prophetic Scriptures.

7. The power for service is derived from the Holy Spirit.

8. The Spirit gives power to believers in order to use them to be witnesses to Jesus Christ.

9. Witnessing to Christ's saving power is the responsibility of only a few Christians.

10. A church should not get involved in foreign missions until it has fully evangelized its own community.

# 2
# FIRST CHURCH AT JERUSALEM
ACTS 2:41-47

## EVERY DAY WITH THE WORD

| | | |
|---|---|---|
| Monday | Profitable for doctrine | II Timothy 3 |
| Tuesday | Fellowship... with His Son | I John 1 |
| Wednesday | This do in remembrance | I Corinthians 11:23-34 |
| Thursday | Prayer was made | Acts 12 |
| Friday | Loving the brethren | I John 2:3-11 |
| Saturday | Rejoice in the Lord | Philippians 4:1-13 |
| Sunday | Ye are builded together | Ephesians 2:11-22 |

**Learn by Heart:**
"Then Peter said unto them, Repent, and be baptized every one of you in the name of Jesus Christ for the remission of sins, and ye shall receive the gift of the Holy Ghost" (Acts 2:38).

Obedience—to some a ridiculously outdated concept, to others the epitome of character.

Lord Nelson is said to have cautioned a young officer, "You must always implicitly obey orders without attempting to form any opinions of your own respecting their propriety."

And a missionary once commented, "For a long time we looked for a word for 'obedience'—a virtue that the tribal people never practiced." The missionary continued to explain that one day he called his dog, and the animal responded at top speed. A tribesman observing this commented, "Your dog is all ear." Finally the missionary had his word—to obey is to be *all ear!*

Christians need to be "all ear" when it comes to God's commands. The Master's instructions to the disciples were clear: "Tarry ye in the city of

In the Word of God, obedience is commanded (Deuteronomy 13:4); however, without faith obedience is impossible (Hebrews 11:6). Obedience is to be from the heart (Romans 6:17), unreserved (Joshua 22:2,3),

18

and constant
(Philippians 2:12).

Jerusalem, until ye be endued with power from on high" (Luke 24:49). When would this power be given? "But ye shall be baptized with the Holy Ghost not many days hence" (Acts 1:5). Jesus Christ did not reveal the precise time of the Spirit's coming. But the disciples waited in obedience. They were "all ear."

## THE CHURCH AND ITS CONVERTS
### (Acts 2:41)

See Leviticus 23:1-22 for the full account of the law governing the feast of Pentecost.

The Jewish nation celebrated the feast of Pentecost fifty days after the "morrow after the sabbath, from the day that ye brought the sheaf of the wave-offering; seven sabbaths shall be complete: Even unto the morrow after the seventh sabbath shall ye number fifty days" (Leviticus 23:15,16). It was on this day marking the close of the harvest season that the Jewish men were to offer new sacrifices unto Jehovah. In order to do this all the males in Israel had to present themselves before the Lord. And since Jerusalem was the center of all religious life in Israel, the men of Israel had to journey to Jerusalem for this sacred day.

Compare Exodus 23:17 with Exodus 34:23 and Acts 2:5.

Since participation in the feast of Pentecost was the sacred obligation of the Jews, it is quite possible that all Jewish believers in Jesus Christ considered this an opportunity to come to Jerusalem and fellowship with other believers. Therefore it is reasonable to assume that many believers besides the 120 who gathered in the upper room were in Jerusalem on the day of Pentecost.

Acts 2:1,2

As these 120 believers were gathered in the house, they were startled to hear what sounded like a tempest. To add to the mystery of it all, they saw a strange fiery phenomenon. A slender tongue like a flame rested upon each believer. They were all filled with the Holy Spirit and "began to speak with other tongues, as the Spirit gave them utterance." The promise of God was fulfilled. The Holy Spirit, the Comforter, had come!

Following this empowering by God's Spirit, Peter faced a hostile crowd and began to preach. These were the same people who had crucified the Lord of glory just fifty days before. Yet, under the Spirit's control, Peter preached a brief but masterful message. He clearly set forth Jesus Christ, crucified and risen from the dead, as the Saviour.

Peter's audience was smitten with heavy conviction from God. In their misery and need, many cried out, "Men and brethren, what shall we do?" (Acts 2:37). Peter replied, "Repent, and be baptized every one of you in the name of Jesus Christ for the remission of sins, and ye shall receive the gift of the Holy Ghost" (verse 38).

Peter emphasized repentance, baptism, remission of sins, and regeneration. Notice, however, that baptism was not the means of securing the remission of sins. The original Greek word translated "for" indicates "at" or "because of." It has the same meaning as "for" in the sentence, "He was congratulated for his success." As the congratulations were a result of his success, so baptism was to be a result of the remission of sins. Baptism was to be an outward, public confession of Christ and of the fact that one's sins were already forgiven through faith in Him.

Baptism has no sacramental value; nor is it a

Acts 2:3,4

The Holy Spirit did not descend upon the believers because they prayed. He came because He was promised to them. See John 14:16,17,26; 16:7,13.

means of salvation. But, it is one of the two New Testament ordinances for the church, and it is important that every believer be baptized in keeping with the injunction of God in Matthew 28:19,20. Baptism is a symbol of the death, burial, and resurrection of Jesus Christ, and of the believer's identification with Him in those three areas. It ought to be the joy of every Christian to be immersed and to give public testimony of his salvation from sin.

What were the results of Peter's preaching? Acts 2:41 tells us, "Then they that gladly received his word were baptized: and the same day there were added unto them about three thousand souls." Sinners joyfully welcomed the gospel as the answer to their spiritual needs. Their faith in Christ Jesus was real. And the grammar of this passage indicates that they received the Word of God *once and for all*. They did business with God and the result was changed lives!

These converts testified publicly of their salvation by being baptized. In all, three thousand souls were added to the already impressive number of believers. This, in the light of Acts 2:47—"And the Lord added to the church daily such as should be saved"—marks the beginning of the organized life of the church.

## THE CHURCH AND ITS CHARTER
### (Acts 2:42-47)

"And they continued stedfastly in the apostles' doctrine and fellowship, and in breaking of bread, and in prayers" (Acts 2:42). Pentecost was marked by a real, lasting, continuing work of God. The new converts continued because they

Critics of immersion have objected to so great a number as 3000 being baptized in one day. But in 1879 at Ongole, India, 2222 "converts were baptized on a single day by six ministers, two administering the ordinance at a time; the services being conducted with all due solemnity, and occupying in all nine hours" (from *A Short History of*

21

were converts of the Holy Spirit. Human persuasion, quiet music, even emotional appeal can often draw a response from some people. But the important thing is that the Spirit of God does a work in the souls of hearers.

*the Baptists*, by Henry C. Vedder).

After the Holy Spirit works in a heart, the new believer needs some guidelines to follow in his new life. A constitution or charter of a political society is a statement of those principles intended for its government. And the charter of the church—the sole authority for matters pertaining to faith and life—is the Word of God. The local church is to be governed by the standards and principles of the New Testament. For this reason Bible doctrine is of the greatest importance to every Bible-believing Christian and church.

II Timothy 3:16,17

The converts of Acts 2 were taught doctrine. They learned the fundamental principles of the faith which the apostles accepted. The apostles were loyal to the truth of God and were dedicated to establishing the new believers in the Word of God.

Acts 2:42

Times have changed, but God's plan hasn't changed even one iota. The teaching of doctrine should still be a vital part of the ministry of every church. For without the fundamentals of the faith there can be no real growth in individual believers. The tendency in recent years to soft-pedal the teaching of Scripture indicates that the greatest need of our churches is the teaching and practice of sound doctrine. There are far too many Christians who don't know what they believe or why. They seem to have forgotten that Paul wrote, "Study to shew thyself approved unto God."

II Timothy 2:15

A church may be large, but it can still be weak

II Peter 3:18

In connection with the Lord's Supper read and study Matthew 26:26-29; 28:19,20. See also I Corinthians 11:23-31.

This is the blessed hope of the Christian (John 14:1-3; I Thessalonians 4:13-18; Philippians 3:20,21; Titus 2:11-13; I John 3:2,3).

in terms of Bible knowledge and spiritual insight and power. If a church substitutes pep for power and pulpit tidbits for Bible lessons, it cannot be well-taught and spiritually mature. But the early believers paid close attention to God's Word, and they grew in grace and knowledge.

The early Christians were obedient to all the commands of Jesus Christ, including the command to observe the Lord's Supper. This ordinance is a memorial of the death, burial and resurrection of our Lord Jesus Christ. When we observe it, we are looking forward to the time when Jesus Christ will return for His own. This is, of course, the believer's hope. And it is truly gracious of God to draw our attention from the world scene with its wickedness, violence, and confusion, and point us to the moment of Christ's coming when we will be glorified in His presence.

Only the born-again Christian is invited to partake of the Lord's Supper. Furthermore, a Christian needs to be in a right relationship with God before he comes to the Lord's table. If an unsaved person or a Christian who is out of fellowship with God comes to the Lord's table, he is indulging in the rankest kind of hypocrisy.

The church of the first century depended greatly upon prayer. God can do much through the church that prays. And yet, how often the prayer meeting is neglected by Christians. Perhaps this is because real praying is hard work. We often talk about prayer, but talking is not enough. Even teaching the blessings of the prayer life is not sufficient. Individual Christians and groups of believers must *participate* in prayer before they can experience God's power.

God answered the early believers' prayers by giving wonders and signs to authenticate the message of the church. The reason for this is the gospel was being preached to Jews, who often demanded a sign from God. Therefore, the Holy Spirit gave signs and wonders that would impress these Jews with the validity of the gospel message.

Hebrews 2:1-4

An intense love prevailed in the church at Jerusalem. Believers sacrificed their possessions and treasured resources, and with these assets met the needs of the less fortunate members in the Christian assembly. They gave much because they loved much.

One who claims to love, yet selfishly takes all he can get, does not know the true meaning of the word "love."

The first-century Christians were extremely grateful to God for the provision He made for their needs, for they "did eat their meat with gladness and singleness of heart" (Acts 2:46). They were constantly praising God (verse 47).

Ingratitude, a flagrant sin, is characteristic of the end time according to II Timothy 3:1-4. Today many believers fail to give God praise for His bountiful blessings. Do you pray aloud before eating when you are home? Do you pause with head bowed for a moment of thanksgiving when you eat in public? This in itself can provide a testimony for the Lord.

Except for the grace of God, we would all be paupers, both physically and spiritually. We need to be ever conscious of what we deserve. This will make us truly thankful for what we have so freely received.

The charter of the church is the New Testament. In this treasured book you will see those principles which are intended by the Spirit of God to govern, energize, and prosper the church. But our churches will be New Testament churches only in proportion to their conformity to the charter and concepts of the churches of Acts.

## NOW TEST YOUR KNOWLEDGE

*Answer true or false:*

1. The people grudgingly received the Word of God.

2. At Peter's insistence, the new converts kept their faith a secret.

3. Baptism is a recent innovation.

4. The study of doctrine had a special place in the early church.

5. Only saved persons are to participate in the Lord's Supper.

6. The early believers saw no need for a lifestyle different from their previous lifestyle.

7. The local church is the only church spoken of in the New Testament.

8. The Holy Spirit did not come as a result of the disciples' prayers.

9. There may have been more than 120 believers in Jerusalem on the day of Pentecost.

10. Peter declared that baptism was necessary for salvation.

## FOOD FOR THOUGHT

*"It is the whole business of the whole church to preach the whole gospel to the whole world."*
—Charles Haddon Spurgeon

# 3
# EARLY CHURCH GROWTH

ACTS 3:1—4:4,14—5:16

---

## EVERY DAY WITH THE WORD

| | | |
|---|---|---|
| Monday | If a man desire the office | I Timothy 3 |
| Tuesday | Take heed unto thyself | I Timothy 4 |
| Wednesday | O man of God | I Timothy 6 |
| Thursday | A workman that needeth not to be ashamed | II Timothy 2 |
| Friday | Called to preach | Jeremiah 1:4-10 |
| Saturday | Full proof of thy ministry | II Timothy 4 |
| Sunday | Perfecting the saints | Ephesians 4:11-16 |

**Learn by Heart:** "Neither is there salvation in any other: for there is none other name under heaven given among men, whereby we must be saved" (Acts 4:12).

John Bunyan, the author of *The Pilgrim's Progress*, was once a cursing, rough, brawling man. But at the age of twenty-eight he accepted Christ as his Lord and Saviour. Soon it was apparent that John Bunyan fervently loved Christ, for he gave every evidence of being a transformed man.

A friend suggested to Bunyan that he become a preacher. He had no formal education, but preach he did, and with great power. On one occasion, in 1660, he was supposed to preach at a farmhouse. But a warrant had been issued for his arrest, so his friends urged him to flee. He could preach later, they reasoned. He turned on his heels, made one trip around the farmhouse, and returned to preach. Bunyan told the amazed

Had not John
Bunyan been
imprisoned, we
would not have
one of the classic
works of litera-
ture, for it was
while he was in
prison that he
wrote The Pil-
grim's Progress.

congregation, "By no means will I run away. I will not stir, neither will I have the meeting dismissed. Come now, be of good cheer. Our cause is right. We need not be ashamed of it . . . we shall be well rewarded if we suffer for it." Little did John Bunyan know that his suffering would include twelve long, weary years in prison.

## POWER AND PROGRESS
### (Acts 3:1—4:4)

The world of Christ's day was no more sympathetic to Christianity than was the world in Bunyan's lifetime. The forces of opposition in Palestine in the time of the early church included Herod Antipas, the son of Herod the Great (Acts 4:27). This was the man Jesus had referred to as "that fox" (Luke 13:32). He was the one to whom Pontius Pilate sent Jesus for trial. Pilate, who had become the Roman procurator in A.D. 26 and was in office during the days of our Lord's ministry, continued his rule until A.D. 36. And Caiaphas, one of Christ's fiercest enemies, con-tinued to be the high priest of the Jews until A.D. 36. So we see that when the young church began its ministry at Pentecost it faced the same political and religious leadership which pre-viously had proved to be antagonistic toward the Lord Jesus. Therefore it is no surprise that the Christians faced persecution.

Use your con-
cordance to look
up passages that
tell of Caiaphas'
treatment of
Christ.

After Pentecost there was a rapid increase in the number of believers in Jerusalem. The Spirit of God was upon the church, and day by day believers went forth to witness of Christ's resur-rection. Thousands were coming to know Christ. All this could not help but excite the hatred and

Make a list of
verses in Acts
that indicate the
growth of the
early church. See
your concordance.

27

bigotry of the Jewish religious leaders. As they had previously plotted the death of the Lord Jesus and madly shouted out their contempt as He hung upon the tree, so now the same leaders plotted to destroy the young church and its apostolic leadership. Against the same political background and amidst the same religious overtones Jesus had ministered in, the young church labored. The same Satanic animosity that struck at the Lord Jesus struck fiercely at the early church.

The enemies of the cross were further incensed by a miracle that Acts 3 reports. A man of over forty years of age who had been lame from birth was miraculously healed. This man, who was totally unable to walk, was fortunate enough to have concerned friends who carried him daily to the temple. There, at the Beautiful Gate, he begged. Perhaps those passing by on their way to worship in the temple would feel some compassion and give him a few alms. Or if they were not compassionate toward him, they might feel obligated to help him anyway, since so many people were watching.

One day, as Peter and John were entering the temple, the lame man implored them to spare just a few coins for him. The apostles had compassion on him and instructed him to look at them. The man's hopes were aroused, for most people merely flipped a coin his way, not wishing to look upon his sad condition. "These men must be different from all the rest! Perhaps they will give me a large sum of money instead of a mere pittance!" But then his hopes were dashed to the earth as the Apostle Peter spoke: "Silver and gold have I none" (Acts 3:6). They wouldn't help him

The Beautiful Gate was probably on the east side of the temple area, at the north end of Solomon's Porch. It overlooked the valley of Kidron and the Garden of Gethsemane. The gate was built by Herod the Great out of Corinthian brass with bas-relief lily work.

Remember that the Pharisees gave alms only so that they would receive men's

28

praise (Matthew 6:2).

after all. But wait—what was Peter saying? "In the name of Jesus Christ of Nazareth rise up and walk" (verse 6). "Jesus of Nazareth—He's the Man who healed the multitudes. Could it be? Yes, I believe He can heal me, too!" As Peter reached for the man's right hand and helped him stand, the man felt a surge of strength rushing to his ankles and feet. He began leaping and praising God. He went into the temple with the apostles, still shouting praise to Jehovah for the miraculous change in his life.

Peter had no material wealth, but what he possessed, he was willing to give. And, as a result, a man's life was transformed.

How many impotent lives are we raising up and transforming into walking, running, leaping Christ-honoring believers? We may not have sufficient resources to give material goods to people, but we have the life-giving gospel of Jesus Christ. We alone possess the power that can save people from eternal darkness. Will we stretch out our hands to others, encouraging them to walk in Christ?

What a blessing it would be if every adult Sunday School class adopted some plan for reaching the lost. Projects to reach the unsaved are feasible for all of us—tract distribution, telephone evangelism, street services, support of missions, jail and hospital meetings, visitation programs for the church and the Sunday School. The opportunities are almost endless.

Acts 4:1-6

## PRAYER AND PROGRESS
### (Acts 4:14—5:16)

The Jewish court could not deny the healing of the man who had been lame from birth. In fact, the court admitted the miracle. But such miracles posed a dangerous threat to them. So the religious leaders spent many hours plotting the course they should take against the preachers who had performed the miracle. They could neither deny nor destroy the power of the gospel; therefore they sought to silence the messengers of the gospel.

You may wonder why the Jewish court did not seek to put Peter and John to death at this time. There were good reasons for their hesitance, all for the benefit of the Jewish leaders. A case against the apostles would have to come before Pontius Pilate, and Pilate was hardly in a mood for hearing such a case only a few months after the crucifixion. The Jewish leaders were not desirous of upsetting any of the Roman authorities, so they decided not to try to have the apostles executed at this time. Also, since the Christian ranks were growing rapidly, there would be a great public outrage should the apostles be sentenced to death. Again, the Jewish leaders were fearful, so they dismissed the apostles with a warning not to preach again.

> The spread of Christianity across the Roman Empire, in the face of heated opposition, was a definite miracle.

Did the apostles go out and immediately resign their commission because the work was too hard, too dangerous, too time-consuming, and too difficult to adjust to? Never! They immediately went to a prayer meeting, because they believed in the power of prayer. The church called upon God, and as they prayed, His power came upon them afresh. Then the preachers went out once again to proclaim the resurrection of Christ.

> Prayer can change the program of a church and make it a soul-winning institution (Acts 4:23-33).

The Word of God stresses the unity of the members of the early church. This was a unity that exists only among those in whom the Holy Spirit of God dwells. There are actually two kinds of unity in the church. First, there is a *basic* unity among believers. All believers belong to the same spiritual family and are a part of the body of Christ. Then there is a *practical* unity which ought to exist among all believers. We should fellowship together in the bonds of peace. Our lives are to be

> True Bible-believing groups will shun efforts at ecumenism, which is distinct from unity.

Our local churches certainly ought to be characterized by practical Christian unity. Church quarrels are detrimental to the church, to the individual families in the church, and to the community.

How many believers today would give all they have to help a brother in Christ?

Romans 12:1

practical expressions of the oneness which is ours in the Spirit. This was true of the believers in Jerusalem.

Acts 4:32-37 points out the love that characterized the church at Jerusalem. Some of the saints had suffered great losses for Christ's sake. To meet their needs, others in the church sold their possessions and set aside the funds to relieve the distress of the saints.

Acts 5:1-11 demonstrates God's demand for purity in the local church. The church must not allow sin to blur the true image of Christ before an unsaved world. Therefore God demands holiness in the lives of His people. When Ananias and Sapphira allowed sin to creep into their lives, God severely disciplined them.

It was the practice of believers to sell their possessions, and to place the funds in a common treasury which met the needs of all who suffered loss for Christ's sake. Ananias and Sapphira sold a possession, kept back a part of the sale price and presented the rest to the Lord by bringing it before the apostles. Peter points out that their keeping some of the money was their privilege (Acts 5:4). But, although they brought only a part of the sale price, they pretended to bring the entire amount and present it to God. This was deception and fraud. So God took their lives, making an example of them.

Sometimes we commit the same sin Ananias and Sapphira committed. We withhold some part of our lives from God while affirming our total surrender to Him. Yet God is patient with us, waiting for us to confess our sin and present our bodies totally to Him.

The church at Jerusalem, loyal and courageous,

full of faith and love, dependent on the Spirit, and fervent in prayer, multiplied under the blessing of God (Acts 5:12-16). Miracles demonstrated the validity of the gospel, and the frontiers of unbelief were pushed back by the power of God.

In the early church it was normal for Christians to live so as to make Jesus Christ attractive to others. No wonder the world took notice of Christians as they manifested the life of Jesus Christ. Let us look to the early church as our model. If we follow the example they set for us, we will receive abundant blessings and will see many come to know Christ as their Lord and Saviour.

God has revealed His Son to us so that we may reveal Him to others.

## FOOD FOR THOUGHT

*"Nothing blinds men to the real character of sin, as the fact that it is their own. Whenever a man is ready to uncover his sins, God is always ready to cover them."*
—Anonymous

*Answer true or false:*

1. Peter and Andrew were going to pray in the temple.

2. A lame man begged at the Sheep Gate.

3. Peter was unable to give the beggar any money.

4. Peter told the lame man, "Take up your bed and walk."

5. The Jewish leaders denied the healing.

6. The apostles were warned not to preach anymore.

7. When the church met for prayer God gave them great power.

8. The church at Jerusalem was unified.

9. Ananias and Sapphira robbed God, so He caused their death.

# 4
# FIRST STEPS IN ADMINISTRATION
ACTS 6:1-7

## EVERY DAY WITH THE WORD

| | | |
|---|---|---|
| Monday | Being many, are one | Romans 12 |
| Tuesday | To every man to profit | I Corinthians 12:1-11 |
| Wednesday | Have the same care | I Corinthians 12:12-31 |
| Thursday | The people murmured | Exodus 17 |
| Friday | She was leprous | Numbers 12 |
| Saturday | Ensamples to the flock | I Peter 5 |
| Sunday | Speak not evil | James 4 |

Learn by Heart: "For as we have many members in one body, and all members have not the same office: So we, being many, are one body in Christ, and every one members one of another" (Romans 12:4,5).

Five-year-old Lisa was nearly overcome with joy. Her sky blue eyes fairly sparkled with excitement, and she wore the biggest smile you can imagine. Her mother was letting her pick any flower in the whole garden, just to make her bedroom prettier! Of course Lisa rushed straight to the roses, which were her favorite. The beautiful colors, the wonderful smell—she could hardly decide which one she wanted. Then she saw it—the perfect flower for her room. The brilliant red blossom looked as if it had been made just for her. She eagerly reached forward, and thrust her hand around the stem. Then she let out a shriek of pain. Thorns! That perfect bloom wasn't perfect after all; it had thorns!

The same is true of the early church. We approach the book of Acts with an idealistic attitude, somehow thinking that "back then" the

How like children we often are. We still practice "hero worship" to

a certain extent,
admiring some
things or people
so much that we
convince our-
selves they are
perfect. We need
to keep our eyes
where they
belong—on Jesus
Christ, the only
truly perfect One
(Hebrews 12:2).

church was untouched by problems. But then we see that even our model for all New Testament churches wasn't trouble-free.

## THE PROBLEM STATED
### (Acts 6:1)

In pointing out the fact that the early church faced certain problems, we do not want to leave the impression that the church was *full* of problems. But there were definite problems, including an undertone of discontent (Acts 6:1).

Churches today also experience difficulties. And this problem of discontent, especially, is one that could give birth to many other problems. Then all the difficulties together could easily destroy the work of the church and its testimony for God. Therefore we should never minimize the seriousness of dissension in the church, but should always be aware of the battles that can come about as a result of what seems to be a minor problem.

Notice that the
cause of the
problem is clearly
set before us.
Most problems
can be handled
more intelligently
if the causes are
known.

"And in those days, when the number of the disciples was multiplied, there arose a murmuring of the Grecians against the Hebrews, because their widows were neglected in the daily ministration" (verse 1). It doesn't take long for problems to appear in churches. Young churches are often full of problems, and the church leadership must proceed with extreme care. But in this instance the situation did not develop until the church had multiplied. By this time the church in Jerusalem was comprised of thousands of members.

Acts 2:44,45;
4:32,34-37

The early Christians were extremely conscious of their responsibilities to care for the poor people in the church, especially the widows. But some widows were not being properly taken care of. Grecian widows were being habitually neglected.

Grecians (Hellenists) were Hebrews who lived outside Palestine. They had taken upon themselves the customs of the Greeks and spoke the Greek language. This was especially offensive to the Hebrews living in the Land who conformed to the Hebrew customs and spoke Hebrew or Aramaic. Consequently, deep prejudices prevailed between these two groups of Jews.

Even though many of these people had become Christians on the day of Pentecost (Acts 2:9-11, 37-41), the rivalry between the Grecians and the Hebrews continued to manifest itself. The Hebrews were discriminating against the Grecian widows in the daily distribution of food and other material items. Consequently the Grecians began complaining and gossiping about the Hebrews. They refused to go to the Hebrews and settle the problem. Instead, they started an undercurrent of dissension.

With the growth of churches come dangers and threats to the spiritual life and power of the assembly. Murmuring, dissension and discontent can do what persecution cannot accomplish. The ungodly spirit of dissension had crept into the church at Jerusalem, and it had to be dealt with in an emergency session of the congregation.

## THE PROPOSED SOLUTION
(Acts 6:2-7)

The apostles did not appoint a committee to handle the problem. Instead, they called a business meeting of the entire congregation.

Paul called the Corinthians carnal, partly because of their dissensions (I Corinthians 3:1-3). This condition can cause endless trouble in churches.

Dissensions are contrary to the unity of Christ (I Corinthians 1:13;12:13). They are contrary to the desire of Jesus Christ for His own (John 17:21-23). And they are contrary to the purpose of Christ (John 10:16).

"Then the twelve called the multitude of the disciples unto them, and said, It is not reason that we should leave the word of God, and serve tables" (verse 2). In calling the congregation together, the apostles planned to deal with what was an evident lack of organization. They saw beyond the immediate problem and sought to meet the real need of the church.

When the believers were assembled, the apostles explained that it was not satisfactory or fitting that they should leave or neglect the ministry of the Word of God and give their time and energies to temporal matters. So they suggested to the members of the church: "Look ye out among you seven men of honest report, full of the Holy Ghost and wisdom, whom we may appoint over this business. But we will give ourselves continually to prayer, and to the ministry of the word" (verses 3,4).

Although the apostles still had authority, they chose to initiate action that would provide a pattern of administration in the churches of the future. Their plan was placed before the congregation for its consent. Seven men (deacons) were to be chosen by the congregation. Scripture does not explain why the number of men to be chosen was seven. The apostles evidently felt that seven were enough to serve the needs of the thousands in the church.

From the very beginning deacons were to be men of character. In Acts 6 we see they were to be known in the community as honest men. They were to be Spirit-filled believers. And they were to have good, practical common sense. In later years Paul gave a more comprehensive statement of qualifications for the office of deacon. Today the

Many people think that having human organization means that we are not trusting God fully. But God is a God of order (I Corinthians 14:33,40).

See I Timothy 3:8-13.

37

office of deacon is an established part of the administration of the local church.

With the appointing of the seven men who would take care of the material needs of the church members, the apostles would be able to devote themselves more fully to the ministry of the Word and to prayer. This should be a guideline for pastors today. They need to spend a great amount of time in Bible study and prayer.

II Timothy 2:15; Ephesians 6:18

The congregation was pleased with the apostles' proposal (verse 5). They chose seven men to serve as deacons. The method they used to choose set a precedent for churches of all time. The word for "choose" means to select with the outstretched hand. Therefore it seems obvious that the church membership took a vote and finally decided on seven deacons.

One interesting thing to notice is that at least two of the deacons, Stephen and Philip, were also preachers of the Word. This shows that participating in a spiritual ministry does not violate the deacon's office. Today deacons not only perform duties in temporal matters but often assist the pastor in spiritual matters as well.

A deacon needs to be spiritually mature in order to help the pastor in spiritual matters in the church.

After the church in Jerusalem took action on the apostles' wise proposal, several problems in the church were solved. First of all, the dissension probably ceased, since the deacons would now have the responsibility to see that no one was neglected. The apostles were relieved of temporal duties and therefore able to devote themselves more fully to the Word of God and prayer. The church continued to grow; and even a company of the priests in Jerusalem was brought to faith in Jesus Christ.

Acts 6:7

Looking back over the first six chapters of the

book of Acts, we notice certain great principles—principles that are intended to characterize the beliefs and practices of all New Testament churches. The membership of the local church is to be a baptized (immersed) membership. Since only believers in Jesus Christ are to be baptized, this precludes the practice of infant baptism. Believers are to partake of the Lord's Supper, which is a memorial of Christ's death, burial, and resurrection, as well as an anticipation of His return. Churches are to be congregational in their government, with issues being decided upon by the vote of church members. Each local church is to be independent and autonomous, following the guidance of the Holy Spirit.

All of these principles are rooted in the New Testament. They are time-tested, God-honored principles and privileges. And they are the heritage of today's churches, bringing blessing to all who practice them.

**FOOD FOR THOUGHT**

*"A true prayer is an inventory of wants, a catalogue of necessities, a revelation of hidden poverty. When you feel most unfit to resort to God you may still go to Him, for He is your fitness and your physician."*
—Charles Haddon Spurgeon

## NOW TEST YOUR KNOWLEDGE

*Answer true or false:*

1. "Grecians" is another word for "Gentiles."

2. The widows should have received food every day.

3. A deacon had to be wealthy.

4. The deacons in the Jerusalem church were lukewarm Christians.

5. The apostles let the church make their own decision about electing deacons.

6. The apostles rebuked the Grecians at the church business meeting for their murmuring.

7. The church in Jerusalem grew slowly as a result of persecution.

# CHRISTIAN WITNESS EXTENDED
### ACTS 8:1-8,26-40

**Learn by Heart:**
"Now then we are ambassadors for Christ, as though God did beseech you by us: we pray you in Christ's stead, be ye reconciled to God"
(II Corinthians 5:20).

## EVERY DAY WITH THE WORD

| | | |
|---|---|---|
| Monday | If the world hate you | John 15:15-27 |
| Tuesday | Ye shall be scattered | John 16:16-33 |
| Wednesday | I pray for them | John 17 |
| Thursday | We glory in tribulations | Romans 5:1-11 |
| Friday | Persecuted, but not forsaken | II Corinthians 4 |
| Saturday | Approving ourselves | II Corinthians 6 |
| Sunday | Handling reproach | Matthew 5:1-12 |

When we think of the stream of graduates from the Bible institutes, Bible colleges and seminaries of our day, we can praise God for every trained, Bible-believing man and woman graduated. However, if each one does not possess a passion for souls, all their time, expense, and investment fall short of God's goal. It is true that pulpits will be filled and the ranks of missionaries will be increased. But what will be the advantage if the men and women lack a God-given passion for souls? If our churches, pastors, officers and lay people do not possess a hunger to see men saved by the grace of God, then we are simply playing church. We will make little impression upon human hearts.

## PROGRESS THROUGH PERSECUTION
## (Acts 8:1-8)

A prominent preacher of God's Word once stated, "All our plans, purposes, and objectives in all departments should culminate and eventuate in leading lost souls to Christ. Teachers and leaders should major in drawing the gospel net, and the spirit of soul-winning should pervade and permeate all. Thus we will have perennial evangelism." What a glorious expression—"perennial evangelism." This is evangelism that lasts all year long, year after year, unceasing, never failing, always fresh. This was the evangelism of the early church.

So far as we can discern conditions in the early church, it seems that it would have been unusual to find a believer who was not fired with zeal to bring others to a living faith in Jesus Christ. What lessons we can learn from these early Christians who counted the privilege of evangelizing dearer than life itself! This love for the lost, this passion for souls, is part of our fabulous spiritual heritage.

The first seven chapters of Acts focus on the church at Jerusalem in the midst of miraculous growth. By the end of Acts 7 there were thousands of members of this great church, certainly enough members to evangelize the world in their day. They were not carnal; they had not lost their joy; they were growing with great strides; but all their work was confined to the Jerusalem area. It seems they had forgotten the commission of Acts 1:8. What about Judaea, Samaria, and the uttermost part of the world? The members had a vision for their immediate area, but it appears they were

Every Christian will stand at the Judgment Seat of Christ to give an account of his labors (I Corinthians 3:9-15; II Corinthians 5:10). Have you considered what your record before Him will be in that day?

Growth in numbers is one experience; growth in grace is quite another. Evidently the church at Jerusalem grew in numbers as well as in the grace of God. Spiritual growth is normal to the

42

healthy Christian (II Peter 3:18). The Scriptures promote growth in the grace of God (I Peter 2:2). The Corinthians were rebuked for remaining babes in Christ (I Corinthians 3:1-4). The Christians addressed in Hebrews 5:11-14 were chided because they should have developed into teachers; but they were still babes in Christ. How much have we developed in Christ?

overlooking the rest of the task, as outlined in Acts 1:8.

Then Stephen preached his memorable sermon in Acts 7. It so enraged the Jews that they thrust him outside the city wall and hurled stones at him until he was dead. This noble deacon became the church's first martyr. But the Jews' anger was not fully placated. They imprisoned, beat, and put to death many who followed the Lord. Soon the fires of persecution drove believers out of Jerusalem to other places in Judaea and as far as points in Samaria. But wherever they went these believers preached Christ and led many to saving faith in Him.

There is every reason to believe that, while believers were engaged in burying the body of the first Christian martyr, Saul was already engaged in making havoc of the church. The persecution of the church is described as "a great persecution" (Acts 8:1) and in verse 3 it is said to have been so fierce that havoc was made of the church at Jerusalem. The original form of the word translated "havock" means to outrage, to tear into pieces as a wild beast would do. With cruel hatred and organized precision, Saul set himself to destroy the church at Jerusalem.

With the persecution of the church came a transition in its ministries. Prior to this time all efforts were Jerusalem-centered. Now the gospel began to radiate outward. There was a spiritual shift in the program of the church. Judaea began to feel the gospel impact. And even despised and shunned Samaritans were now receiving the Word of God.

Philip, another deacon, stepped into the place left by Stephen. His subsequent ministry to the

Samaritans was attended by the working of miracles, the salvation of many, and great joy experienced by all who came to know the Lord. All the walls of prejudice and bigotry were broken down by the gospel. The events of Acts 8:9-17 constitute ample proof that God granted the Samaritans full spiritual privileges and status, equal to what the Jews at Pentecost received and equal as well to what was later given to the Gentiles in Acts 10 and 11.

Jesus had once met the need of a Samaritan woman and in so doing crossed the social barriers of His day (John 4).

## PROGRESS THROUGH PREACHING (Acts 8:26-40)

"And the angel of the Lord spake unto Philip, saying, Arise, and go toward the south unto the way that goeth down from Jerusalem unto Gaza, which is desert" (verse 26). God called Philip away from a busy and successful time of evangelism in Samaria. Great faith was required for him to instantly obey the will of God, for Philip might have questioned God's leading in his life. Or he could have called God's attention to mighty successes in Samaria. But he did not do this. Obedience to the known will of God was something of a spiritual adventure to Philip. And it still is. The loyal servant of Christ obeys God even though he may not know the way or God's immediate purposes.

God leads the prepared worker to the prepared heart for witness. Do you begin each day with a prayer that God will lead you to that heart He has prepared for your witness?

"And he arose and went: and, behold, a man of Ethiopia, an eunuch of great authority under Candace queen of the Ethiopians" (verse 27). In verses 27-29 it becomes clear why God directed Philip to the Gaza area. The Ethiopian eunuch was a man of great political stature. He had charge of all the treasure of the queen. Luke

Joseph and Daniel are examples of Jewish men who held positions of authority in Gentile lands.

records the fact that his purpose in coming to Jerusalem was to worship; therefore we know this man was interested in Judaism. And perhaps he was even a Jew by birth, for his position was that generally given to a Jew in the government of a foreign power.

On the other hand, he could have been a Gentile, an African who had become a *proselyte* to Judaism. At any rate, he possessed at least a portion of the Old Testament, for he was engaged in reading Isaiah as he rode along the desolate way. The Holy Spirit directed Philip to make contact with this soul in need.

The eunuch had been reading Isaiah 53, so Philip immediately took up where the Ethiopian had left off his reading. From Isaiah 53 Philip preached Jesus Christ crucified and risen. Who can say how long the sermon lasted? It has been suggested that, if the Ethiopian had not interrupted Philip with a question about his baptism, Philip might have preached the whole way back to Ethiopia!

In the course of the journey the chariot came to a certain body of water. It caught the eunuch's eye. Obviously Philip had sought to impress the eunuch with the need to be baptized as a public testimony of his faith in Christ. Baptism is a symbol of the death, burial, and resurrection of Christ Jesus. So public baptism is the means of heralding one's faith in Christ and his identification with Christ in death, burial, and resurrection. Philip was a faithful witness; he had declared the full Christian responsibility to this new convert to Christianity.

See Matthew 28:19,20; Romans 6:4,5.

The words, "See, here is water; what doth hinder me to be baptized?" (verse 36) are followed by Philip's immediate examination of the Ethiopian concerning his faith in Jesus Christ as the Son of God, and obviously as his personal Lord and Saviour (verse 37). If his faith was firmly rooted in Christ, then he could be baptized, and it could happen immediately.

To think that a man of such high rank in the Ethiopian government would travel alone is untenable. He must have traveled in a caravan with attendants. One can see him call the caravan to a halt and gather all his attendants and friends to the water to witness his confession of Jesus Christ as the Son of God and his Saviour. He was baptized, and with this act of bold obedience to his Lord, the eunuch sealed his testimony. All else had been renounced for the sake of Christ.

The eunuch continued on his way, and no doubt became the first herald of the gospel in Ethiopia. As for Philip, he was caught away and went to Azotus (the Philistine Ashdod). He then worked his way north along the coast from city to city until he came to Caesarea.

The baptism of the Ethiopian eunuch highlights several important truths. First, baptism's Scriptural mode is immersion. Acts 8:38 indicates that Philip and the Ethiopian "went down both into the water." Obviously, there would not have been any need for both of them to enter the water if sprinkling had been an acceptable mode. Philip could have just scooped up a handful of water to sprinkle on the Ethiopian's head. Secondly, baptism should be administered to believers only. Philip refused to baptize the Ethiopian without the assurance that the Ethiopian had indeed believed on Christ. Third, baptism is a privilege. "If thou believest with all thine heart, thou

Believer's baptism by immersion is distinctive of the New Testament. It is not optional; it is part of obedience. In this respect the eunuch shames many professing Christians. As a newborn babe in Christ he already knew his responsibility.

If this is so, then Philip had a ministry even greater than the one he could have had by continuing in Samaria. Think of giving Africa the gospel! How good to leave the choices in God's hands!

*mayest*," Philip told the Ethiopian. Every believer should recognize how highly privileged he is to identify himself publicly in baptism as a follower follower of Jesus Christ. Why, then, do some believers wait so long to be baptized? Finally, obeying the Lord in baptism is an act which brings joy to the one who gets baptized. The baptized Ethiopian believer "went on his way rejoicing" (verse 39). If you haven't been baptized yet, the Ethiopian's question to Philip is one you need to ask: "What doth hinder me to be baptized?" (verse 36).

The progress of the church continued. Jerusalem, Judaea, Samaria, Ethiopia, and now Gentile Caesarea. Caesarea was a strategically important city with a large Gentile population. The Gentiles, too, must hear the good news. So Philip made his home in Caesarea (Acts 21:8), and his four daughters were likewise engaged in a witness for Christ. A man who could take Stephen's place and introduce the gospel to the Samaritans, the Ethiopian, and the Gentiles of Caesarea was a mighty man of God and wonderfully endowed by the God of all grace.

**FOOD FOR THOUGHT**

*"An opportunity to do good is the same as a command to undertake the work."*
—Anonymous

## NOW TEST YOUR KNOWLEDGE

*What do you say?*

1. Would you say Saul's religious zeal and fervor fueled his fanatical persecution of the church? Cite a Scripture. _____

2. Was Saul's persecution of Christians in any way related to a refusal to face his own problems?

3. In what points did Stephen and Philip resemble each other as servants of God? _____

4. What would you say are some qualifications for successful soul winning? (Acts 8:26-40)

5. What are some procedures of soul winning? (Acts 8:26-40) _____

6. How would you describe the eunuch before his salvation and after? _____

*Answer true or false:*

7. It is more important to be courageous in soul winning than it is to know the Scriptures.

8. It is important to be friendly and as personable as possible to be a successful soul winner.

9. The soul winner should show the new convert his spiritual responsibilities.

# THE GREATER WITNESS
## ACTS 9:1-19; 11:1-18

### EVERY DAY WITH THE WORD

| | | |
|---|---|---|
| Monday | Hebrew of the Hebrews | Philippians 3 |
| Tuesday | Gamaliel's student | Acts 22:1-16 |
| Wednesday | A Pharisee | Acts 26:1-29 |
| Thursday | Appeal to Caesar | Acts 25:10-27 |
| Friday | Taught by grace | Titus 2:11-15 |
| Saturday | Made alive | Ephesians 2:1-9 |
| Sunday | Established | Psalm 40:1-5 |

One wonders how many believers ever prayed for Stalin, Hitler and other tyrants of history. It would probably require many pages to tell why we often neglect to pray for such persons. Do you think that the early Christians prayed for Saul of Tarsus? He was arrogant, hostile, and fanatical, yet God convicted Saul and Saul trusted Christ. It should not surprise us if we learn in Heaven that some of the early Christians entreated God for this man's soul.

### THE CONVERSION OF SAUL
### (Acts 9:1-19)

It was not God's will that the blessings and privileges of the gospel be limited to a Jewish church. True, the converts at Pentecost were

Jewish. And the first seven chapters of Acts deal with the church at Jerusalem, comprised of converts from Judaism. However, this was intended by God to be only a beginning. Acts 1:8 speaks of Jerusalem as a point of beginning in terms of witness for Christ.

There was a tendency for the church at Jerusalem to "hoard" the gospel. Apparently no step had been taken prior to Acts 8 to extend the gospel in the direction of the Gentiles as Acts 1:8 prescribes. Perhaps this failure grew in part out of the national background of the Jerusalem church members. In Acts 8 the fires of persecution burned fiercely, and the church was scattered. Thus the witness of the gospel was carried into Judaea and Samaria. Philip was selected by God to present the Word of God to the Ethiopian eunuch. In a little while the gospel was being transported by chariot right into Africa. The gospel was on the march!

But the task was only in its infancy! Much remained to be done by way of setting the stage for the ministry to the regions beyond. The one central man in God's plan for world evangelism was yet to be redeemed. Saul of Tarsus still needed to hear and believe the gospel. God would mightily use Peter, but first He had to break down Peter's strong Jewish prejudice. Our lesson concerns itself with both steps—Saul's conversion and Peter's instruction at the hands of God. When these steps were taken, the gospel target was enlarged and the mighty purposes of the Lord moved forward to victory.

The difficulties faced by the early church are in part expressed in the words, "And Saul, yet breathing out threatenings and slaughter against

In the Word it is clear that God's servants are separated (Acts 13:2; Galatians 1:15); chosen (John 15:19; Acts 9:15; I Corinthians 1:27); gifted (Romans 12:6; I Corinthians 12:8); sustained (Acts 18:10; Philippians 4:13-19); crowned (I Peter 5:4; James 1:12; II Timothy 4:8).

the disciples of the Lord, went unto the high priest, and desired of him letters to Damascus to the synagogues" (Acts 9:1,2). Saul's hatred for Christians caused him to pursue them at every turn. If his life was to be changed, it would obviously require the power of God. But then—is not the gospel of Christ "the power of God unto salvation"? (Romans 1:16). History reveals that the gospel has changed the greatest of sinners!

Think of the Scotsman, Geddie, who went to evangelize island people in the New Hebrides. They were, at that time, savage cannibals. On Aneitym an inscription was placed over Geddie's grave: "When he came to the island in 1848, there was not a single Christian; when he left in 1872 there was not a single heathen." This testimony demonstrates the mighty power of the gospel. And this message was sufficient for the spiritual needs in the life of Saul of Tarsus.

Do you think that believers ever prayed for Saul of Tarsus? If they did, it would have appeared that their prayers were not being answered. Things were becoming worse for the church, and of course Saul was often the instigator of their trouble. Persecution previously centering in Jerusalem was reaching out to new areas. The circle of inquisition was becoming larger, and Saul, filled with rage, now moved against Christians in Damascus. The days were becoming harder and harder for believers.

Damascus was a fairly large city about 120 miles northeast of Jerusalem. It boasted a Jewish population around 40,000 and possibly contained as many as forty synagogues. We know there were believers in Damascus because Saul journeyed there to apprehend them. It is possible that there

Do not cease to pray for loved ones and others who seem to grow harder in their attitude toward Christ.

You may wonder if Saul was not the real power behind the persecution, rather than the high priests. Of course, the high priest would have to give Saul his commission to apprehend the Christians, thus

51

were Jews from Damascus in Jerusalem at Pentecost who had heard the gospel, believed, and returned to Damascus. And, of course, the persecutions of Acts 8:1-4 scattered Christians. Probably, some of them moved as far north as Damascus. The witness of the Christians in Damascus undoubtedly resulted in the multiplication of their numbers. At any rate, their witness and numbers were of sufficient importance to attract the attention and wrath of Saul of Tarsus.

Saul was completely consumed by his passion to destroy Christians. He lived in and breathed an atmosphere of hatred, violence, and even murder. He took the initiative, went to the high priest, and requested authority to do the dastardly thing he proposed against the church at Damascus (Acts 9:1,2). His desire was granted.

Saul and his party left Jerusalem to travel the 120 miles to Damascus. As they neared the gate of the city, suddenly a great light, greater than the midday sun, flashed around them, and they all were stricken to the earth. His companions heard only a noise, but Saul heard the words of the risen Christ, "Saul, Saul, why persecutest thou me?" Bewildered, Saul respectfully inquired, "Who art thou, Lord [Sir]?" Then came the answer, "I am Jesus, whom thou persecutest: it is hard for thee to kick against the pricks" (Acts 9:5).

This answer fell upon Saul's soul with life-changing power. Jesus Christ had touched a tender spot in Saul's life. The word "pricks" (Greek, *kentron*) means goads, instruments made by inserting a sharpened piece of iron into a stick. Oxen were prodded with goads, and often the animals kicked back as though to attack the

legalizing their abuse and even murder.

The high priest was either Jonathan or Theophilus, sons of Annas, who both occupied this office.

Acts 9:3-5

irritant. "Kicking against the goads" became synonymous with being rebellious in spirit.

One wonders what contributed to Saul's deep conviction. Certainly it was conviction of sin, and as always, this was the work of the Holy Spirit of God. But no doubt there were other factors that contributed to his inward rebellion. Perhaps Stephen's death had had a sobering effect upon Saul. Stephen had died triumphantly, in the demonstration of a victorious faith (Acts 7:54-60). Howbeit, Saul was under conviction, and a man under conviction is prone to bold and wicked conduct and language.

John 16:7-11

Most tenderly Jesus asked, "Saul, it is painful for you, isn't it, as you kick back against the goads in rebellion?" There in the dust of the Damascus road the proud, self-righteous Saul was broken by the power of God. As he lay there, he believed on Jesus Christ crucified and—as he now well knew—risen from the dead! It is no surprise that Saul rose with fear and amazement and inquired, "Lord, what wilt thou have me to do?" (Acts 9:6). This was submission to the will of God, and it characterized the new Saul of Tarsus from that moment forward. Also, it ought to be the controlling desire of every Christian. Saul's conversion resulted in his complete surrender to the lordship of Jesus Christ, a surrender that influenced the whole of his life and labors.

Workers for God must be competent (I Chronicles 9:13; 12:33); diligent (Ezra 7:23; Nehemiah 4:21); trusting in God for results (Nehemiah 4:11-14).

Taken to the house of Judas, Saul was met there by Ananias, who laid his hands upon him. Ananias spoke assuringly to Saul, and through God's miraculous power, restored sight to Saul's eyes (Acts 9:8-17). Saul arose in the strength of his new life, was baptized as a public confession of Christ, and was received into the fellowship of the church at Damascus (verses 18,19).

God was at work here in preparation for the greater witness of the church to the ends of the earth. The conversion of Saul was a mighty step in that direction, but there were others yet to come. One of these steps was the preparation of the Apostle Peter and the church at Jerusalem.

It is the will of God that the gospel be taken to the ends of the earth. This plan is given in Acts 1:8.

## THE CONVERSION OF CORNELIUS
## (Acts 11:1-18)

Peter continued to exhibit Jewish attitudes and conduct even after the events of Pentecost. As far as we know from the record, the church at Jerusalem was totally Jewish in its membership through the first seven chapters of Acts. How could they overlook God's plan as given in Acts 1:8? We don't know. The truth of Christianity should have led them to know that all men who believe on Jesus Christ become one in Him. Nevertheless, preparation was necessary in the lives of Peter and the church leaders at Jerusalem if they were to participate in gospel testimony to the Gentiles.

Peter lived "many days in Joppa with one Simon a tanner" (Acts 9:43). One wonders how this experience affected his Jewish sensitivities. Little did he know that to the north in the city of Caesarea God was at work in the life of a Roman military commander, a centurion of the Italian division of the imperial Roman army. Cornelius was an unregenerate Gentile, but he sought light in spiritual matters and evidently lived up to the light he had already received. Instructed by God in a vision, Cornelius sent to Joppa for Simon

Acts 10:1-8

Peter, for "he shall tell thee what thou oughtest to do" (Acts 10:6).

Peter later recounted the fact that at the same time God was instructing him with regard to Cornelius and his need. It was clear that God intended for Peter to preach the gospel to Cornelius and his house—"Who shall tell thee words, whereby thou and all thy house shall be saved."

Acts 10:6; 11:14

Acts 10:9-16

To instruct and impress His Jewish disciple, the Lord gave Peter a vision. He lowered a vessel from Heaven—a vessel filled with beasts, creeping things and fowls. God instructed Peter to slay and eat. But this brought Peter's immediate refusal on the grounds of his strict observance of Jewish law. No common food—nothing unconsecrated—had ever entered Peter's mouth. In spite of his protests, though, Peter was confronted by the revelation that these dietary laws had been done away with. These laws were not binding upon the Christian living and serving God in the new dispensation. "What God hath cleansed, that call not thou common" (verse 9).

Leviticus 11:2-27; Deuteronomy 14:3-20; Acts 11:1-10; Matthew 5:17; Galatians 3:24-29.

Acts 10:23ff

Peter's word to Cornelius upon his arrival at Cornelius' home indicates that he got the point—"God hath shewed me that I should not call any man common or unclean" (Acts 10:28). No man is to be excluded from a gospel witness simply on the basis of who or what he is! If he is a sinner, he needs the witness. This is the lesson Peter learned in the vision from God. And so, too, we need to be careful to share God's good news with those around us, regardless of who they are.

Acts 10:34,35

## NOW TEST YOUR KNOWLEDGE

*Answer true or false:*

1. By the time of Stephen's death in Acts 7 the gospel blessings had been extended to Jew and Gentile alike.

2. It is possible that Stephen's death had a serious effect upon Saul of Tarsus.

3. Saul of Tarsus believed he was serving God by persecuting the church.

4. Saul of Tarsus was destined to be a vessel to bear the gospel of Christ to the Jews.

5. Peter was instructed by God in a vision because he was prejudiced against the Gentiles.

6. Peter learned that no man is rejected by God because of his ethnic or social status.

*Underscore the correct words:*

7. Saul's conviction by the Holy Spirit is best seen in the fact that: 1) he served on the Sanhedrin; 2) he consented to Stephen's death; 3) he made havoc of the church.

8. Cornelius was saved: 1) solely by grace; 2) through alms-giving.

## FOOD FOR THOUGHT

*"I would think it a greater happiness to gain one soul to Christ than mountains of silver and gold to myself."*
—Matthew Henry

# 7

# GROUNDWORK FOR WORLD VISION
## ACTS 11:19-30

**Learn by Heart:**
"Yet if any man suffer as a Christian, let him not be ashamed; but let him glorify God on this behalf" (I Peter 4:16).

### EVERY DAY WITH THE WORD

| | | |
|---|---|---|
| Monday | Shun fables | I Timothy 1 |
| Tuesday | Sound words | II Timothy 1 |
| Wednesday | "God of truth" | Deuteronomy 32:1-6 |
| Thursday | Obey the Word | Psalm 119:1-9 |
| Friday | Sent to preach | Romans 10:1-17 |
| Saturday | Doers of the Word | James 1:13-27 |
| Sunday | Milk of the Word | I Peter 2:1-8 |

*Persecution:* What a dreaded word! But millions of believers all over the world are suffering persecution for taking a stand for Christ. They would rather be true to their Saviour than save themselves. Thousands of Christians are in jeopardy every time they meet for worship, for their actions are against the desire of the government.

Yet in Western culture people tend to neglect their Christianity for such trivial things as entertainment, material possessions, and worldly activities. Perhaps God will have to bring severe persecution to the Western world to bring Christians into a closer relationship with Himself. He brought persecution to the early church to get them to fulfill their responsibilities of witnessing in other parts of the world. But once He allowed those early believers to suffer for His name, they

Acts 1:8

received abundant blessings and experienced phenomenal growth.

## THE CHURCH AT ANTIOCH
## (Acts 11:19-26)

"Now they which were scattered abroad upon the persecution that arose about Stephen travelled as far as Phenice, and Cyprus, and Antioch, preaching the word to none but unto the Jews only" (verse 19). This verse takes us back about eight years to Acts 8:1-4—to the days of dreadful persecution at the hands of Saul of Tarsus. Those were dangerous days, when no believer could consider himself safe from Saul the persecutor. It cost much then, sometimes even life itself, to stand up and be counted as a believer in Jesus Christ.

The church at Antioch was born because believers had been driven out of their homes for Christ's sake. Wherever they went, they preached the gospel, souls were saved, and churches were established. But no church was destined to influence the history of the world as greatly as the church at Antioch. It was a brilliant light in a morally darkened world.

The founders of the Antiochan church were burdened for the needs of Jews and Gentiles alike. The fact that the church had both groups in its membership shows that evangelism had reached into both segments of the city's population. However, it is interesting to notice that when the first preachers of the Word came to Antioch, they declared the gospel to the Jews only. Then, those who followed, men of Cyprus and Cyrene

Would you stand for God in the face of persecution? Could God count upon you?

Antioch was located in Syria on the Orontes River. It was the third largest city in the Roman Empire, being surpassed only by Rome and Alexandria.

(Acts 11:20), declared the Word to the Grecians (Gentiles).

In the meantime the almost unbelievable thing had happened! Saul of Tarsus, the bitter enemy of the Christian church in that day, was on his way to Damascus when Christ met him. Saul acknowledged Christ as his Lord and followed His instructions to go to Damascus. After being baptized, Saul stayed with the disciples in Damascus for a short time. Then he went into Arabia for a three-year retreat (Galatians 1:17,18). Later he came to Jerusalem, where Barnabas gave him support and encouraged the believers to accept him as one of their own.

No doubt Saul was trained by God in the desert as Moses was trained for forty years on the backside of the desert (Exodus 3).

Acts 10; 11

Another step in the progress of the church at Jerusalem was made when Peter made his memorable journey from Joppa to Caesarea to meet with Cornelius and his family. Through Peter's witness Cornelius was born again, received the Holy Spirit, and was baptized. When Peter bore testimony of these mighty events to the apostles and leaders in Jerusalem, they were satisfied that now God had granted repentance to the Gentiles.

Many were saved as a result of the witness to the Gentiles in Antioch. "And the hand of the Lord was with them: and a great number believed, and turned unto the Lord" (Acts 11:21). They turned away from their sin and idols to embrace Jesus Christ and His salvation.

Compare Acts 11:21 with the experience of the Thessalonians (I Thessalonians 1:9,10).

News like this could not be contained. Revival was going on in the city of Antioch. When tidings of these things reached Jerusalem, the church thought it proper to commission Barnabas to help teach the Word of God in Antioch.

Remember that the first deacons were elected by the church (Acts

We first see Barnabas as a believer, a Levite

from Cyprus who had been won to Christ (Acts 4:36,37). He possessed qualities that ought to grace the lives of all Christians: "For he was a good man, and full of the Holy Ghost and of faith: and much people was added unto the Lord" (Acts 11:24). On the basis of the last statement in verse 24, we may conclude that he was a dynamic soul winner. He was also quite generous, as we see in Acts 4:37.

6). The church again made a choice and sent Barnabas forth to Antioch as their ambassador (Acts 11:22).

Barnabas was filled with the Holy Spirit, and therefore his total life and labor were under the sovereign control of the Spirit. He was motivated and energized by the Spirit, and Jesus Christ was manifest in all areas of his life. He was also full of faith. This means he believed in a God who was able to do the impossible, and he trusted Him to do the impossible. Thus, Barnabas was a source of great inspiration and strength to the church at Antioch.

Suppose the church in Jerusalem had sent a man to Antioch who was not an outstanding Christian? Would the church at Antioch have become the great spiritual giant it was with its exemplary missionary outlook?

Barnabas rejoiced in all that the Lord had accomplished in the church (Acts 11:23). He did not credit men with the results, for he knew that God had given the increase. But Barnabas also saw that the young believers were still in great need of pastoral care, and he urged them to pursue a life of fellowship with the Lord Jesus Christ.

Leadership in our churches is of first importance to the life of the church. Spirit-filled men, full of faith, are necessary to develop a church into a driving force for God. See I Timothy 3:1-13; 4:13-16; II Timothy 2:15-26; 4:1-8.

However, the work was great—too great for one man. Help—trained help—was needed. So Barnabas made a journey to Tarsus where he found Saul. Saul realized the great opportunity to serve the Lord, so with God's permission he accompanied Barnabas to Antioch.

For one year Barnabas and Saul instructed the young church at Antioch in the Word of God. Evidently the believers assembled publicly (verse 26), and no doubt there was a good attendance at all the meetings. Lives had been changed, and believers were being strengthened, and this was the best possible advertising for the church.

It was at Antioch that believers in Jesus Christ were first called "Christians." It is not clear in Scripture whether or not this term was first used in a derisive manner. But it did serve to associate one with Jesus Christ. And in due time believers came to use it universally to identify themselves.

Do you give proper time to Bible study? Second Timothy 2:15 sets forth God's desire for the Christian's relationship to the Word of God. See also Psalm 119; II Timothy 3:16,17.

## THE CHURCH IN ACTION
### (Acts 11:27-30)

Prophets often came from Jerusalem to Antioch to minister. One prophet named Agabus indicated that a great dearth (famine) was to come upon the entire empire. And when the famine did come, it touched the lives of believers and non-believers alike. Christians are not immune to trouble. Some Christians entertain the mistaken notion that being saved magically frees them from all difficulties. Sometimes, however, problems *multiply* when a person becomes a believer; yet every Christian may take every problem and need to Jesus Christ and receive grace to help (Hebrews 4:16). Earthquakes, floods, fires, typhoons, hurricanes, sickness and a variety of other troubles can reach believers in this work-a-day, live-a-day world. But we have access to the throne of God, and there we can express our needs, no matter what those needs may be. Our God answers prayer.

Saints in the hill country of Judaea and Jerusalem were experiencing a famine which had risen to serious proportions. How was this critical problem to be met? With no hesitation the young church at Antioch gathered together whatever would meet the needs of the Judaean saints. Every man gave according to his ability, for this is God's method. God does not approve of a few believers carrying the responsibilities of the whole church, as so often happens today. Joyfully these believers at Antioch gathered their substance. They placed their offering in the hands of Barnabas and Saul so that it could be taken to the elders (the overseers or pastors) in Judaea. The church of Antioch not only received abundant blessings from God, but they rejoiced in being able to give to others.

Since giving characterized this church in Antioch, it is not surprising that in a short time the Holy Spirit called upon them to send forth men from their number. He called Barnabas and Saul to carry the gospel to multitudes in desperate spiritual need. The young church responded to God's bidding because they had, first of all, given themselves to Him. A church will not give in the manner God instructs unless it has first of all settled the question of dedication to Jesus Christ.

God uses men, not angels, to preach the gospel of His redeeming grace. To declare the Word of God is one of the highest of all privileges. To put oneself at God's disposal to be used as He sees fit is a mark of obedience to God. To serve God in

Christian stewardship is a privilege. We should give of our substance according to our ability so as to glorify God (II Corinthians 8:1-15; 9:6-15; Philippians 4:19).

"It is more blessed to give than to receive" (Acts 20:35).

Acts 13:2

Isaiah 6:8

His place, in His time, and in His way is a mark of genuine spiritual success.

## NOW TEST YOUR KNOWLEDGE

*Answer true or false:*

1. Agabus was a Roman centurion.

2. Barnabas was of the tribe of Benjamin.

3. At first the gospel was preached in Antioch to Jews only.

4. Barnabas was a member of the Jerusalem church.

5. Barnabas was a dynamic soul winner.

6. The Jews refused to accept Peter's claim that God was saving Gentiles.

7. The word "Christian" applied only to the apostles.

8. The church in Antioch gave aid to the church at Jerusalem.

9. Many of the believers in the church at Antioch would not give to the famine victims.

10. Paul started the church at Antioch.

## FOOD FOR THOUGHT

*"Faith in its operations towards the ultimate Christian character will discover a wide range for its activity. It will aid in the production of humility, patience, confidence, calmness and quietness."*

—Walter J. Main

# 8
# FIRST MISSIONARY ENDEAVOR
ACTS 13:1-13; 14:23-28

## EVERY DAY WITH THE WORD

| | | |
|---|---|---|
| Monday | Silver and gold idols | Psalm 115 |
| Tuesday | Send me | Isaiah 6 |
| Wednesday | I send | Matthew 10 |
| Thursday | A great harvest | Luke 10:1-12 |
| Friday | From darkness to light | Isaiah 9:1-7 |
| Saturday | Ambassadors for Christ | II Corinthians 5:14-21 |
| Sunday | Children of light | I Thessalonians 5:1-10 |

**Learn by Heart:**
"To open their eyes, and to turn them from darkness to light, and from the power of Satan unto God, that they may receive forgiveness of sins..." (Acts 26:18).

With energy conservation receiving so much attention, our thoughts are often on power. How can we get more power? Will solar energy solve our problems? Or is nuclear energy the answer? Power is so necessary to everyday life, yet is becoming more difficult to come by.

What a contrast in the life of a Christian! He has limitless power dwelling inside him. The Creator of the universe is ready and waiting for each believer to utilize the power He has to offer. Such infinite power cannot be measured in terms of watts or horsepower. It can be evaluated only by its results.

## THE WORKERS CHOSEN
(Acts 13:1-4)

The power of the gospel has changed the lives ‖

No matter how
deep in sin a man
may be, he is not
a hopeless case
(Romans 1:16).

of individuals and families, and has even altered
the course of whole cities and nations. In fact, the
gospel of Christ changed the course of human
history in the Middle East and Europe. The
historical triumph of the gospel in Asia and
Europe can be traced back to a prayer meeting
held in the church at Antioch in Syria when five
men laid hold upon the power of God.

"Now there were in the church that was at
Antioch certain prophets and teachers; as Barnabas, and Simeon that was called Niger, and
Lucius of Cyrene, and Manaen, which had been
brought up with Herod the tetrarch, and Saul"
(Acts 13:1). We are familiar with Barnabas and
Saul. But we know virtually nothing about
Simeon, Lucius, and Manaen. We do know they
were prophets and teachers. But they didn't spend
all their time in teaching, for they knew there was
a time to pray. They realized that the greatest need
at this particular time was for them to raise their
voices in petition to the Lord.

Are you inclined
to neglect your
prayer life? Do
you ever feel, as
you honestly take
stock of your life,
that you are more
interested in
study, in teach-
ing, in going
somewhere for
God, than you are
in prayer? Prayer
is work, but it is
our most urgent
need.

When the accounts are all in, and believers
stand before the Judgment Seat of Christ, it will
doubtless be revealed that God kept a very careful
record of those who prayed. In answer to the
petitions of prayer warriors the power of God has
often fallen upon a local church or other
Christian work. Behind the great revivals of
history and the great periods of evangelistic fervor
and success, there have been those who have
prayed with power. These people may have been
"unknowns" as far as other believers were concerned; but *God* knows them because they
prayed.

Scripture doesn't reveal what the five men in
the church at Antioch in Syria were praying

about. Perhaps they prayed for great population centers like Antioch in Pisidia. And can't you hear Barnabas earnestly, fervently praying for his homeland, the island of Cyprus? God responded to their prayers. He reached down and tapped Barnabas and Saul on the shoulder. "I want you to go. I have a work for you to do for me in the regions beyond."

Do you pray for your neighbors? God may answer those prayers by sending *you* to your neighbors with a witness. Do you pray for New Guinea, the West Indies, Pakistan, Brazil? God may send *you* or your son or daughter. If you are honestly praying for God's will to be done, you must be willing to respond to His leading.

"Separate me Barnabas and Saul for the work whereunto I have called them" (Acts 13:2) are words these men of God would never forget. God called them by name and stated that He had a specific work for them to do—they were to be foreign missionaries. But God didn't indicate that this work was more important than any other service for Him. Some Christians have elevated foreign missionary service to the degree that all other Christian service seems to be unimportant. They reason that a believer needs a definite call to serve the Lord in Africa or India, but not to be a teacher in the Sunday School, a deacon in the church, a secretary, or a treasurer. They often forget that God has a specific place for *every* believer as a member of the body of Christ. And God *calls* every believer to the work He has for him. Perhaps you have refused to teach a class either because you do not consider it important enough, or because you want to keep yourself open until that one really "big" opportunity

God called Moses to a specific work, as revealed in Exodus 4:1-16; He also called Aaron (Psalm 105:26; Hebrews 5:4), Joshua (Numbers 27:18-23; Joshua 1:1-9), and Gideon (Judges 6:11-16).

comes along. Remember, though, teaching two-year-olds or cleaning the church building *is* a big task if it is the task God has for you.

Don't be guilty of refusing the call of God to the place of His choosing. God knows where you can be used to the fullest extent and where you will glorify Him the most.

The church at Antioch recognized God's call of Barnabas and Saul. So being led by the Holy Spirit, they gathered for a commissioning service and sent the men out to serve God (Acts 13:3). In reality the Holy Spirit sent them forth, for He moved through the church to perform His gracious purposes.

"So they, being sent forth by the Holy Ghost, departed unto Seleucia; and from thence they sailed to Cyprus" (verse 4).

## THE WITNESS EXPANDED
### (Acts 13:5-13; 14:23-28)

"And when they had gone through the isle unto Paphos, they found a certain sorcerer, a false prophet, a Jew, whose name was Bar-jesus: Which was with the deputy of the country, Sergius Paulus.... But Elymas the sorcerer... withstood them, seeking to turn away the deputy from the faith" (Acts 13:6-8).

Elymas, a servant of Satan, saw the interest Sergius Paulus had in the gospel preachers and their message. So he attempted to harass Paul and Barnabas in order to turn Sergius Paulus away from God. Paul did not mince words. He came straight to the point, calling Elymas "thou child of the devil, thou enemy of all righteousness" (verse 10). Paul knew an enemy of God when he saw

Satan chooses to operate through men. He performs his evil through those who suit his purposes. He sought to hinder Sergius Paulus through an openly declared sorcerer. At times one, and he also knew it was time for action!

Paul stood before the sorcerer and boldly called down the judgment of God upon him. And gradually, but surely, Elymas was blinded by a stroke of God's hand.

The power of God was so obvious that the proconsul "believed" and was amazed at the teaching of the apostles. We do not know whether or not Sergius Paulus actually became a Christian. The word "believed" does not necessarily indicate faith in Christ. Remember that Acts 8:13 tells us Simon the sorcerer "believed" and was even baptized. Yet Peter said to Simon, "Thou hast neither part nor lot in this matter: for thy heart is not right in the sight of God." As far as Sergius Paulus is concerned, Scripture does not state that he had a genuine conversion experience. But we like to think that when God struck Elymas with blindness, He also released Sergius Paulus from Satan's grip and the man was truly born again.

Days of rigorous travel, preaching and teaching, persecution and suffering followed as the two missionaries visited Perga, Antioch in Pisidia, Iconium, Lystra and Derbe, and then made the trip home to Antioch in Syria. As they covered the many miles of their journey, they left behind them organized churches. They didn't stop with just a witness and a "God bless you," but made sure the new believers were well established in the Word. And they helped the congregations select elders to oversee the assemblies.

Upon arriving back home in Antioch of Syria Paul and Barnabas called the church together and "rehearsed all that God had done with them, and how he had opened the door of faith unto the

he deceives by appearing as an angel of light (II Corinthians 11:13-15).

See Acts 8:13-23.

It is interesting to notice that at Paphos Saul of Tarsus laid aside his Hebrew name and assumed his Roman name, Paul. J.C. Macaulay says, "Doubtless Paul had both names previous to this time ... but it is surely significant that the Hebrew name is dropped and the Roman

Gentiles" (Acts 14:27). They did not discuss how much they had done for God, but what God had used them to accomplish. What we do for God is not so important, but what we trust Him to do through us—that is what really matters. What rejoicing must have filled the meeting place as the missionaries testified of the power of God!

Believers ought to look back and recognize the gracious act of God in calling men to serve Him. Service for Jesus Christ is a privilege, and we must not think of it in any other way. The privilege of service for God is solely by His gracious call. To serve One so great, so glorious as the eternal God of the universe is nothing short of the greatest privilege ever to be conferred upon redeemed man.

Men consider it a great honor to be selected as an honor guard for a state function. Men consider it a great honor to be chosen as foreign ambassadors. And these are great privileges! But what are these compared to being chosen by God to serve Him in proclaiming the gospel? This is a privilege not even extended to the angels of God. And the joy it can bring is unexcelled. Accept God's call; obey His bidding. You'll be blessed abundantly, and you'll have no regrets.

## FOOD FOR THOUGHT

*"To you is given not gold, nor silver, nor precious stones to fashion, but immortal spirits that shall glorify Christ on earth and in heaven."*

—Charles Haddon Spurgeon

## NOW TEST YOUR KNOWLEDGE

*Answer true or false:*

1. The Holy Spirit's only call to Christians is to serve as foreign missionaries.

2. God expects Christians to strive for important positions in the church.

3. Satan uses men to oppose God's work.

4. God sometimes uses a man to answer his own prayer.

5. Saul and Barnabas were sitting around waiting for God to call them to serve Him.

6. Prayer warriors are highly important to the work of God.

7. If a person is "unknown," he is not valuable to God.

8. Paul and Barnabas let the new believers establish their own churches.

9. The apostles rejoiced in what God had done through them.

10. Elymas tried to turn Sergius Paulus away from God.

# FIRST CHURCH COUNCIL DECISION
## ACTS 15:1-29

## EVERY DAY WITH THE WORD

| | | |
|---|---|---|
| Monday | All are under sin | Romans 3:9-31 |
| Tuesday | The righteousness of faith | Romans 4:13-25 |
| Wednesday | Justified by faith | Habakkuk 2:1-4 |
| Thursday | False brethren | Galatians 2:1-14 |
| Friday | Justified by Christ | Galatians 2:15—3:9 |
| Saturday | Our schoolmaster | Galatians 3:13-29 |
| Sunday | The adoption of sons | Galatians 4 |

Satan blinds men to the truth and ensnares them (II Corinthians 4:4; I Timothy 3:7; II Timothy 2:26). The saints of God must beware of Satan, and must always be armed against his attacks (II Corinthians 2:11; Ephesians 6:11-18).

Years ago a Bible teacher was traveling through a midwestern state. As he drove through a small village, a sign over the blacksmith shop caught his eye: "All Kinds of Twisting and Turning Done Here." The man was immediately reminded of his archenemy, the devil. The devil, too, twists and turns. He is violently opposed to the Word of God, and many times it suits his evil purposes to deny the Bible and its teachings. He will not hesitate to do all in his power to strip it of all divine inspiration. However, on occasion he will assent to some degree of inspiration and value of Scripture if it will contribute to his ultimate purposes of destroying faith.

Satan is also a most unusual mathematician. He *subtracts* from the power of the gospel of Christ by *adding* conditions for salvation. He *divides* churches by *multiplying* errors. So when the devil engages in religious blacksmithing or when he begins to figure—look out!

## THE CONTROVERSY
### (Acts 15:1-6)

In the case of the church at Antioch, Satan's methods were quite obvious. His purpose was to destroy the effective witness of that church. It had become the key church in all Syria. It was a gospel-preaching center. Its beams of the gospel message stretched out over the troubled seas and rocky shoals of Syria. As far as Satan was concerned, the light must be put out! And how would he accomplish such wickedness? By twisting the gospel of redeeming grace into what was no gospel at all.

How did the devil present to the church at Antioch a totally new—actually perverted—concept of salvation? Men came from Jerusalem, without the authorization of the church there, and taught the brethren in Antioch that circumcision was absolutely necessary to salvation. They agreed that faith was important, but in addition to faith in Jesus as the Messiah, obedience to the Law of Moses was necessary.

Perhaps these men came to Antioch and held a public meeting. Or maybe they quietly held a special study group or Bible class in one of the homes and invited others of the church for a little "fellowship." Satan has often worked that way. And usually, the results have been the same. In due time the saints of God are confused and unsettled, divided and partisan in their beliefs.

The enemy's attack in Antioch was against the very foundations of the church. The plan was to

The church needs to be taught the Word of God. Sound, thorough, doctrinal, practical Bible instruction alone will protect the church from error (II Timothy 3:16,17).

Their message was a bold denial of the adequacy

72

of the cross of Jesus Christ. It was a mixture of law and grace. It confused legalism and sacramentalism with evangelical, life-giving truth.

Galatians 2:3

destroy the message, pervert the gospel, and add to the Word so that it might lose its power. So Satan recruited zealous, sincere, hardworking teachers from Jerusalem to go to Antioch with this false gospel. They were quite convincing in their claim that "except ye be circumcised after the manner of Moses, ye cannot be saved" (verse 1).

Paul, Barnabas, and others in the church openly resisted this heretical teaching. Then it was finally suggested by brethren in the church that a deputation go, at the expense of the church, to the apostles, elders, and the rest of the congregation at Jerusalem. The delegation would consult the Jerusalem church about the matter. So Paul, Barnabas, and others, including Titus, an uncircumcised Gentile, made the journey to Jerusalem.

In Jerusalem the men were "received of the church, and of the apostles and elders, and they declared all things that God had done with them" (verse 4). The group from Antioch was not limited in its approach to the problem by being placed in the hands of a committee or board, for the New Testament churches operated on the principle that true church action is action taken by the entire congregation. The authority of a New Testament church belonged to all its people. It is no surprise, then, to learn that the delegation gave its story to the entire church at Jerusalem.

In any matter of controversy brought before the church the members must be able to hear both sides, for anything less than this is an outright denial of the principles of democratic church government set forth in the New Testament. So the Judaizing party, comprised of ex-Pharisees who had been converted to faith in Jesus as the Messiah, spoke up, saying "that it was needful to circumcise them, and to command them to keep the law of Moses" (verse 5). The council broke up after this presentation, and we see in Galatians 2:2 that the delegates from the church in Antioch used the recess to speak privately with the apostles. Then the entire group reconvened in order to discuss the Judaizers' presentation of their viewpoint.

They were still Jews at heart, and their beliefs made it necessary for the Gentiles to become Jews before they could become Christians.

## THE COUNCIL
## (Acts 15:7-29)

When the council reassembled there was extensive discussion, inquiry, and deliberation, as we see from the word "disputing" in Acts 15:7. This word does not necessarily mean a heated, nasty debate. It does indicate a thorough examination of all sides of the issue. In the middle of this discussion Peter, the apostle to the circumcision, took the floor and addressed the council. Peter's words were of serious importance to the audience. Had he not been in the company of Jesus? And was he not the tremendous preacher of the day of Pentecost? And of course, he was a Jew and had a special interest in preaching the gospel to his Jewish brethren.

Acts 15:7-11

The gospel of the circumcision was committed to Peter (Galatians 2:7).

In Acts 15:7-11 it is clear that Peter made the following points: By the specific instruction and planning of God he had gone to the house of Cornelius to preach the gospel. As a result Cornelius and his household believed and received the Holy Spirit. They spoke with tongues. And they were baptized. God had given his seal of

74

"But we believe that through the grace of the Lord Jesus Christ we shall be saved, even as they" (Acts 15:11).

Galatians 1:19;
Matthew 13:55;
Mark 6:3

James even cited Scripture from the Septuagint—the Greek Old Testament—in support of God's intent to save the Gentiles (Amos 9:11,12).

approval to their faith and to the reality of their salvation. And no one could deny this, for God had dealt with Jews and with Gentiles in the same manner (Acts 2; 10).

Peter also warned the council against provoking God to anger or displeasure by placing upon the Gentiles a yoke of the Law. This was a yoke which not even the Jews or their fathers had been able to bear, so it would be ridiculous to expect the Gentiles to bear it.

The council had been awed into silence as Peter presented his case. When Peter finished, Barnabas and Paul continued where he had left off.

James, the chairman of the council, rose to conclude the session. "Simeon [Peter] hath declared how God at the first did visit the Gentiles, to take out of them a people for his name" (Acts 15:14). Yes, God had indicated His plan to open the door of faith to the Gentiles by first of all giving Peter and Cornelius visions, then bringing them together so that Cornelius and his house might be saved (Acts 10; 11).

As James spoke, the council must have leaned forward to catch every word. His words were designed to render a masterful, satisfying judgment in the matter. James suggested that a letter be written to the church at Antioch to declare that the church at Jerusalem, with its leaders, the apostles and elders (pastors), found absolutely no justification for the view that the Gentiles needed to be circumcised in order to be saved.

On the other hand, fellowship among the Jews and the Gentiles as Christians was of great importance. So, to effect such fellowship, the Gentiles would have to refrain from those practices that would prove offensive to their Jewish brethren.

True Christian love will not deliberately, intentionally give offense to other believers. Christian fellowship and love will forego the enjoyment of, or the exercise of, certain liberties in Christ which might rightfully be ours, if those liberties will offend a brother.

After James gave his suggestion to the council, the church acted and together gave support to what was evident to all as the wisdom of God. With this action the council adjourned. History was made, and the churches in Syria were preserved from the destruction of Satan.

A Christian does not possess liberty without limits. He is only as free as the great principles of Christian living presented in the New Testament permit him to be (I Corinthians 8).

## FOOD FOR THOUGHT

*"Churches must drop many of their 'social activities' in favor of the more urgent tasks. If the church today suffers from any one ailment above others, it is from triviality."*
—The Evangelical Witness

## NOW TEST YOUR KNOWLEDGE

*Answer true or false:*

1. The members of a local church should be willing to meet to conduct the Lord's business.

2. Peter agreed with the Judaizers.

3. Titus was the last speaker at the council.

4. Every church member should hear both sides of a controversial matter.

5. Principles are unimportant when dealing with specific church problems.

6. Barnabas and Paul cited miracles God had shown to the Gentiles.

7. The church does not hold final authority in all matters of decision.

8. The Gentile believers did not have to refrain from offending their Jewish brothers.

9. Salvation is by grace through faith alone.

10. The majority should rule in a church.

# 10
# MISSIONARY WORK BROADENED
ACTS 15:36—18:22

## EVERY DAY WITH THE WORD

| | | |
|---|---|---|
| Monday | Sowing the seed | Psalm 126 |
| Tuesday | A waiting harvest | John 4 |
| Wednesday | Faithful preaching | Acts 20:17-27 |
| Thursday | Gracious invitation | Isaiah 1:1-18 |
| Friday | Faithful Word | Isaiah 55 |
| Saturday | Compelled to preach | I Corinthians 9:7-16 |
| Sunday | Help wanted | Matthew 9 |

A missionary once wrote, "I would that I had a thousand lives and a thousand bodies that I might devote them all to no other employment than preaching the gospel to those who have never heard the joyful sound!" What a noble desire!

What is your highest ambition?

One life seems hardly enough to the truly dedicated Christian as he puts himself at the Lord's disposal for whatever God's will is for him. But the majority of us Christians give only a tiny percentage of what we should give to help spread the gospel message. A missionary statesman challenged believers with this searching question: "Can you place a finger on a single spot on the map of the world and say with joy: 'There I have a missionary for whom I pray, one whom I help to support'?" Missionaries can't do the job alone. Will you help?

Missions ought to be the heartbeat of every church and every Christian.

## NEW WORKERS ENLISTED
### (Acts 15:36—16:3)

The church at Antioch was a nerve center of missionary effort. The Holy Spirit had called faithful men to be His ambassadors to places where Jesus Christ had not been preached. As a result of this missionary zeal, souls had been saved and churches had been established. In due time the missionaries returned to the home base at Antioch. But they did not return to rest. Their lives were busy despite the fact that they had just returned from a time of rigorous service for the Lord. Paul and Barnabas "continued in Antioch, teaching and preaching the word of the Lord" (Acts 15:35).

The test of a church's effectiveness is not whether it involves its members in busyness but in Biblical evangelism and edification.

Notice that Paul and Barnabas taught in the church at Antioch "with many others also" (verse 35). The church was a thriving, growing work for the Lord. Probably "the lights were on" every night in the church. No doubt there was always something important going on, some new truths to be learned, some new converts being strengthened and fortified with the Word.

God calls and directs His servant to the place of His choosing (Acts 13:2,4; 8:26).

Perhaps Paul began to wonder about the number of teachers in this one church. His mind traveled out over the plains and mountains to the north and to the west. He could see Jews steeped in a lifeless religion and Gentiles who were idol worshipers, totally ignorant of the true God. Perhaps he said to himself, "There are enough men to teach and preach the message here in Antioch. It's time to move out to the regions beyond and teach other brethren in the younger churches. And there are others who must hear the gospel of Christ before it is too late." So Paul suggested to Barnabas, "Let us go again and visit our brethren in every city where we have preached the word of the Lord, and see how they do" (Acts 15:36).

Barnabas agreed to this wise proposal. But when it came time to consider who should make up the missionary party, Barnabas and Paul did not see eye to eye. There was a contention between Paul and Barnabas regarding John Mark, Barnabas' young cousin. On the first journey, when Paul and his company had arrived in Perga, John Mark suddenly deserted the party and went to Jerusalem. God does not tell us why he turned his back upon the work, but Paul evidently considered him guilty of wrongdoing. So he decided that John Mark should not accompany them again.

Paul probably reasoned that since Mark had proved to be undependable on the first tour, it would jeopardize the work of the Lord to entrust him again with responsibility. This would be an arduous journey, and it would take great self-discipline. Barnabas evidently wanted Paul to give Mark another chance. But Paul did not wish to take a chance with Mark. In some ways both men were right. But they could not agree, so Barnabas took John Mark and set sail for Cyprus, his homeland.

This was hardly the last instance that two leaders could not serve the Lord together. And unfortunately, the differences between some men have been very great rather than just minor disagreements. Occasionally the Lord's servants will become bitter against one another. And unlike Barnabas and Paul, some never become

*Paul set an example in following up on his spiritual children.*

*In later years Paul was reconciled to Barnabas. He also publicly recognized the work of John Mark (Colossians 4:10; II Timothy 4:11).*

reconciled to each other. This grieves the Holy Spirit and greatly hinders the work of God.

With Barnabas and John Mark out of the picture, Paul still needed to select additional personnel for the missionary party. He chose Silas, a Gentile believer, to accompany him on the journey. God had prepared the way for Paul in this respect, for when Silas came from Jerusalem to visit the church at Antioch, he decided to remain in Antioch despite the fact that others of his party from Jerusalem returned.

The second missionary journey began in A.D. 50, and the missionary party went northward through Syria into Cilicia. They no doubt stopped in Paul's home city of Tarsus, then went on to Derbe and Lystra. Lystra was the home of young Timothy, who lived with his mother, Eunice, and his grandmother, Lois. These three had grown remarkably in the Lord since the first time Paul had been in Lystra.

Timothy was now about nineteen or perhaps twenty years of age. And though Timothy was not physically strong and was somewhat reserved, Paul could see qualities of leadership in the young man. So Paul asked Timothy to accompany the missionary group as the replacement for John Mark.

Timothy's mother was a Jewess, and Timothy's father, who was evidently dead at this time, had been Greek. There is no evidence in Scripture that Timothy's father provided any spiritual training for Timothy. All this responsibility rested upon the two women in the home. So you can well imagine what this call of God to Timothy meant to these godly women. Perhaps they had hoped that young Timothy would be able to serve the

Silas, called Silvanus, is mentioned in I Thessalonians 1:1.

This description of Timothy is based on I Timothy 4:12; II Timothy 1:6-8; and I Timothy 5:23.

Because Timothy was half Jewish Paul thought it wise that he be circumcised so as to avoid offending the Jews.

Lord as a missionary like the Apostle Paul. But whether or not they had foreseen this area of service for him, Eunice and Lois had given Timothy to the Lord. And the hour had finally come for Timothy to answer God's call to full-time service.

The missionary team was on its way. The ministries of the group resulted in the edification of the believers, and the churches were growing in number daily. God added His blessing to the dedicated efforts of the missionaries, and they saw great things accomplished.

Timothy was zealous (Philippians 2:19-22; I Timothy 6:12), powerful (II Timothy 1:6), and dear to Paul (I Corinthians 4:17; Philippians 2:22; I Timothy 1:2,18; II Timothy 1:2-4).

## NEW FIELDS EVANGELIZED
## (Acts 16:4—18:22)

The missionaries worked their way into the Phrygian and Galatian regions, but the Lord restrained them from preaching the gospel in Asia (Acts 16:6). Therefore, they passed *through* Asia. When they arrived at Mysia they planned to turn northward into Bithynia. But the Spirit of God again forbade them to preach (verse 7). It seemed evident to Paul that God wanted him at the seaport of Troas, so he moved out to this coastal city (verse 8).

During the night God gave Paul a vision. A man from Macedonia stood before him and implored, "Come over into Macedonia, and help us" (verse 9). Paul saw this as the call of God to him to go to Europe. Paul followed the Lord's leading, and through the apostle the Holy Spirit directed the missionaries to reach Europe with the gospel of redemption (verse 10).

After Luke, the physician, joined the missionary party at Troas, they sailed to Neapolis (verse

Luke, a follower of Christ, was a

11). Then they walked the eight miles to Philippi (verse 12). Philippi was a great, thriving city, from which Alexander the Great had launched his conquest of the world four centuries before. But a power even greater than Alexander's was to be revealed to the Greeks in the form of the gospel of Christ.

The missionaries' first convert was a woman named Lydia (verses 13-15). She believed on Christ and was baptized. Then, led by God, she prevailed upon the missionary team to accept her hospitality and remain in her home. Thus, God provided for His servants.

Leaving a company of believers behind in Philippi the missionaries moved on to Thessalonica (Acts 16:40; 17:1), where Paul's witness to the Jews and the Greeks resulted in the conversion of a multitude and the establishing of a New Testament church (Acts 17:4). Here Aristarchus, Gaius, Secundus, and others were saved (Acts 19:29; 20:4; 27:2; Colossians 4:10; Philemon 24). But then Paul left suddenly by night for Berea, some fifty miles away (Acts 17:10).

Cicero rightly called Berea an "out-of-the-way" city. Built quite a distance from the sea, it was somewhat free of all the activity of a busy coastal city. It seemed such a peaceful city, for to the south was beautiful Mount Olympus with its snowy top. Here in Berea the missionaries were able to preach to Jews in the synagogue (verse 10). When these Jews heard the gospel message for the first time, they eagerly, diligently searched the Scriptures to verify the missionaries' words (verse 11). Many of these Jews as well as many Greeks presented themselves to the Lord, and very soon a church was formed in Berea (verse 12). When a riot broke out in that city, Paul left for Athens (verse 13-15). But Silas and Timothy remained at Berea, no doubt for the purpose of strengthening the church (verse 14).

Athens, a breathtaking city, surpassed every other city of its day as a cultural center. Architecture, philosophy, the arts—Athenians lived for the enjoyment of these pursuits. But even with all the city's beauty, its citizens were slaves to idolatry (verse 16). The fearful evidences of this paganism were found on every hand. But Paul was faithful, and delivered the truth to the citizens of Athens (verses 17-31). Some of the Athenians mocked Paul's preaching, finding it foreign to everything they had ever heard. Others were impressed (verse 32). And when Paul finally departed from Athens, there were some new members in God's family (verses 33,34).

See Acts 17:15-34. Here in Athens, Dionysius, a Roman official, was saved and Damaris came to know the Lord. Stephanas was the first convert in Achaia (I Corinthians 16:15), and others were saved as the Word was preached with power.

And now Corinth! (Acts 18:1). There was no other city like it among the Greeks for commerce and wealth. It was unique in that it boasted one harbor on the west toward Italy and another on the east toward Asia. It was a commercial crossroads which abounded in wealth. Paul had no support from the outside when he entered Corinth, so he resorted to his trade of tentmaking. He met some believing Jews, Aquila and Priscilla, who were also tentmakers. So the three of them labored together. More than that, this godly couple let Paul live with them (verses 2,3). God had again made adequate provision for His servant. Paul still spent time preaching and teaching to both Jews and Gentiles even while he was working (verse 4). Then Silas, Luke, and Timothy met Paul in Corinth; and through their united ministries, a great multitude believed and were baptized (verses 5-10). A church was established, and the missionaries continued in the great city a year and six months, teaching the Word of God (verse 11).

Over three years had passed since Paul and Silas left Antioch in A.D. 50, intent upon visiting and strengthening the churches. Now Paul evidently left Silas, Luke, and Timothy in Corinth (verse 18). Along with Aquila and Priscilla, he sailed to Ephesus (verse 19). There he bore witness in the synagogue of Jesus as the Messiah. Then, although the people would have detained him, Paul left for Caesarea (verses 20,21). Landing at this Palestinian port, he went up to Jerusalem (verse 22). Imagine the joy with which he related the victories of the Lord to the church and its leaders!

Finally, the apostle arrived in Antioch (verses 22,23). What a reunion with the saints of God! They had grown in the Lord in Paul's absence, bringing joy to the apostle. And in giving his report to the church, Paul's heart must have overflowed with praise as he rehearsed all that God had done. Abundant blessings were upon them all.

It is good to share with our Christian brothers what the Lord has done for and through us. Believers rejoice when they hear of God's working in lives.

## FOOD FOR THOUGHT

*"The men who move the world are the ones who do not let the world move them."*
—Dwight L. Moody

# NOW TEST YOUR KNOWLEDGE

*Underline the correct answer:*

1. Paul cast a demon out of a young woman in: (Athens, Berea, Philippi).

2. Christians were accused of turning "the world upside down" at: (Corinth, Thessalonica, Cyprus).

3. The city of (Athens, Berea, Corinth) was said to be totally given over to idolatry.

4. Mars' Hill was located in the city of: (Philippi, Rome, Corinth, Athens).

5. Timothy's mother was: (Lydia, Lois, Eunice).

6. John Mark was: (Barnabas' brother, Silas' nephew, Barnabas' cousin).

7. (Antioch, Lystra, Philippi) was Timothy's home.

8. Aquila was a: (Roman official, tentmaker, missionary).

9. Barnabas was replaced by: (Silas, Mark, Dionysius).

10. (Priscilla, Lydia, Damaris) was Paul's first European convert.

# THE CHURCHES STRENGTHENED

ACTS 18:23—20:38

## EVERY DAY WITH THE WORD

| | | |
|---|---|---|
| Monday | Saints knowing | Ephesians 1:15-23 |
| Tuesday | Saints walking | Colossians 1:1-19 |
| Wednesday | Saints forgiving | Colossians 3:1-13 |
| Thursday | Saints comprehending | Ephesians 3:13-21 |
| Friday | Saints growing | II Thessalonians 1 |
| Saturday | Saints working | James 2 |
| Sunday | Saints building | I Corinthians 3:1-15 |

People are lost in sin and desperately need to hear the gospel. Read John 3:14-18 and Romans 1:14-16.

"I would rather win one soul for Christ than civilize one million souls without Christ." What a tremendous statement of the truth that man is lost apart from a personal experience with the Lord Jesus Christ! Regeneration, not civilization, is man's deepest need. Paul truly believed this, and his three missionary journeys provide a lasting, eloquent testimony to his love for souls.

In the months following his second missionary tour, Paul cherished his memory of the churches in Asia Minor, Philippi, Thessalonica, Berea, and Corinth. His thoughts were translated into fervent prayer for all the churches, and as he prayed he became conscious of the will of God. He must visit old fields of labor, and he must travel to new ones.

## MINISTRY, MIRACLES AND MOBS
### (Acts 18:23—19:41)

It was the year A.D. 54, and the Apostle Paul set out once again. Time was marching on, and for Paul, who was certainly no longer a young man, this tour would be his last opportunity to visit many of the churches that were dear to him.

It was Paul's custom to reach the great cities in his ministry. These were centers of influence, as are Chicago, Denver, Los Angeles, Montreal, Ottawa, Toronto and other major cities. Paul knew that by reaching such centers of population, learning, commerce, and religion, he would influence the thinking, and even the entire life, of the surrounding towns and villages. The third missionary tour was no exception to this evangelistic emphasis in the great cities. But first of all, upon leaving Antioch, Paul revisited the churches he had helped establish in Galatia and Phrygia. He visited one church after another, strengthening and stabilizing the believers.

While Paul was busy ministering to the churches in the north, something tremendously important was occurring in Ephesus. A visitor who had come to Ephesus from Alexandria in Egypt had attracted much attention. He was Apollos, a Jew. And he evidently deserved the publicity he received, for we see in Acts 18:24-28 that Apollos was "an eloquent man, and mighty in the scriptures" (verse 24). He "was instructed in the way of the Lord; and . . . fervent in the spirit" (verse 25). In other words, it is obvious that this man, Apollos, was an accomplished, gifted, eloquent teacher of the Word of God. But wait— there was something about his ministry that was

Paul's companions on the third journey are not listed for us. However, we know that Timothy continued to travel with the apostle. There is also the possibility that Erastus had traveled with Paul since his first trip to Corinth. And Gaius and Aristarchus may have remained with him following his first visit to Macedonia.

This conveys the idea that Apollos was educated and well-versed in the Scriptures.

not quite right. He knew "only the baptism of John" (verse 25).

This statement clearly indicates that Apollos was ignorant of all that had happened on the day of Pentecost when God ushered in a new age. He knew only John the Baptist's message, and he preached it, calling men and women to repentance and faith in God. He called upon men to be baptized as a token of their repentance and confession of sin. No doubt he honored Jesus Christ to the same extent that John the Baptist had honored Him—as the Messiah, the Lamb of God. But regarding the significance of the cross, the resurrection, the work of the Spirit of God at Pentecost and in subsequent days, Apollos was totally in the dark. The teacher needed to be taught.

God will not allow a spiritual need such as Apollos had to go unfulfilled. He took steps to meet this great man's need. As Apollos ministered in the synagogue in Ephesus, Aquila and Priscilla listened. They realized that Apollos needed to be taught, so they took him aside and instructed him in "the way of God more perfectly" (verse 26).

It was at this point that Apollos proved his true greatness. Although he was certainly a masterful teacher, he was nevertheless a teachable man. So many of God's children who possess great gifts and have great reputations are not teachable. They are of the opinion that they know it all. Even if they were at all inclined to submit to teaching, they probably would not choose such teachers as Aquila and Priscilla, who were "mere" tentmakers. Had Apollos been like so many Christians today, he might have chosen to be taught by Paul himself. Or he may have demanded to be tutored

Aquila, a Jew, was a native of Pontus. Like Paul, he was a tentmaker. He had probably been in business in Rome, but Claudius' edict ordering all Jews out of Rome evidently caused him to settle in Corinth. We do not know when he and his wife, Priscilla, became Christians. But certainly it was before they left Corinth with Paul by a degreed and accredited teacher from Alexandria or Jerusalem. But Apollos did not have this attitude. His head might have been wrong in some respects, but his heart was right. What he lacked, he was willing to learn from whoever could teach him. Aquila and Priscilla filled Apollos in on all that had happened since the ministry of John the Baptist—the cross, the resurrection, the ascension, Pentecost, the church, the door of opportunity and blessing that was now open to the Gentiles as well as to the Jews. He eagerly listened, tested all things by the Word, and believed what these humble lay people had spoken.

When Apollos had learned all Aquila and Priscilla taught him, it was recommended by the believers in Ephesus that he travel to Corinth. And his ministry at the great city in Achaia was indeed a success, "for he mightily convinced the Jews, and that publickly, shewing by the scriptures that Jesus was Christ" (verse 28).

Unfortunately for Apollos, the Corinthians did what God never intended. The Corinthian believers became divided in their loyalties to *men*. Groups formed around Peter, Paul, and Apollos. These divisions in the church weakened its witness and grieved the Holy Spirit. But Apollos is not to be blamed for this situation, for there is no evidence that he fostered the partisanship.

While Apollos was busy in Corinth, Paul completed his tour of the Galatian and Phrygian regions, finally arriving with his co-workers in the city of Ephesus. His first contact upon reaching the city was with twelve "believers." Possibly these men were followers of Apollos who had been baptized by him in his earlier days in Ephesus.

(I Corinthians 16:19). Romans 16:3 refers to them as being at Rome again. However, we know they returned once more to Ephesus, for Paul greeted them during his second imprisonment (II Timothy 4:19).

This practice was condemned by Paul in I Corinthians 1:11-13; 3:5-8.

Paul's question, "Have ye received the Holy Ghost since ye

believed?" means, "Did you receive the Holy Ghost when you believed?" (Acts 19:2).

This was the last of four instances in Acts when the Holy Spirit was given with special manifestations. Every instance was a sign to Jews of the introduction of a new age. (See Acts 2:1-4,38; 8:12-17; 10:44-48; 19:1-7.)

It is obvious that these twelve knew no more than Apollos had known at the time when Aquila and Priscilla began instructing him in the way of the Lord. So Paul taught them in the things of Christ and brought them to see clearly truths about the kingdom. These men had previously been baptized with John's baptism—in repentance and confession of sin, preparatory to Christ's coming. But they now submitted to Christian baptism in full assurance of faith in the crucified, risen, ascended, and coming Saviour.

As Paul laid his hands on the twelve, the Holy Spirit came upon them, and they spoke in tongues as did the Jews at Pentecost and the Gentiles in Caesarea (Acts 2; 10). This was a sign to them, as Jews, that they had been received by God.

Paul continued to minister for three months in the synagogue at Ephesus, reasoning with the Jews. Some of these Jews trusted in Christ, but the majority of them "were hardened, and believed not" (Acts 19:9). They became quite vocal and spoke evil of Jesus Christ before the multitude. So Paul gathered the believers around him, and together they left the synagogue. After finding quarters in the school of Tyrannus, Paul continued to teach Christianity in Ephesus for two years.

The shocking paganism of Ephesus is hard to describe. The worship of the Greek goddess, Artemis (the Roman name for this goddess of fertility was *Diana*), was associated with all the filthiness and vileness so common to pagan worship. Demonism often played a large part in the tremendous hold that paganism had upon the hearts and minds of the ancients. So it is no surprise that God performed mighty miracles through Paul, thus demonstrating that the gospel message was indeed divine, powerful enough to save men from Satan's grip (Hebrews 2:3,4).

## TEACHING, TRAVELING AND TEARS
## (Acts 20:1-38)

Paul's travels took him into Macedonia and later into Achaia. Upon leaving Corinth, he traveled to Asia with a company of Christian leaders. At Troas Luke rejoined the apostolic group. This is indicated by the use of "we" in verse 6.

After leaving Troas, Paul went to Miletus. While he was there he called the elders (pastors) of the church at Ephesus to meet with him. This meeting was a time of tender fellowship between the men who had responsibility over this church and the man God had used to bring it into existence. In the course of their fellowship Paul recalled the ministry God had entrusted to him. He did what so few believers actually dare to do— he called attention to the manner of his life and the consistency of his Christian conduct. But Paul could honestly do this. No one could deny that he had faithfully taught the Word of God.

This blessed time of fellowship impressed the elders that this would be their last meeting with Paul. So, before Paul left, they spent some time together in prayer. They accompanied him to the ship that would soon take him to Palestine. Then they returned to their duties. Workers move on, but the work remains!

It is interesting to learn that Paul's faithful teaching of the Word resulted in the enjoyment of heartfelt fellowship. True Christian fellowship depends on a congregation's love for the Word.

## NOW TEST YOUR KNOWLEDGE

*Answer true or false:*

1. Aquila's wife was Diana.

2. Demetrius was not a believer in Christ.

3. Sceva's sons tried to cast out demons.

4. Eutychus knew "only the baptism of John."

5. Tyrannus baptized the twelve Ephesians.

6. Apollos was a Greek god.

7. The Ephesian elders received instruction from Paul.

8. Aquila and Priscilla instructed Apollos.

## FOOD FOR THOUGHT

*"I have been weakly cheered by a large number of brethren who have greatly sympathized with me and helped me to fight the Lord's battles by bravely looking on!"*
—Charles Haddon Spurgeon

## 12
# GOSPEL WITNESS MAINTAINED
ACTS 21:10—22:24; 23:1-10; 24; 25:1-12; 26

---

## EVERY DAY WITH THE WORD

| | | |
|---|---|---|
| Monday | Win the prize | I Corinthians 9:24-27 |
| Tuesday | Don't quit | I Corinthians 15:51-58 |
| Wednesday | Out of affliction | II Corinthians 2 |
| Thursday | Don't be weary | Galatians 6:1-9 |
| Friday | Don't fear | Psalm 27 |
| Saturday | Don't fret | Psalm 37:1-9 |
| Sunday | Faith on trial | I Peter 1:1-9 |

Learn by Heart: "But sanctify the Lord God in your hearts: and be ready always to give an answer to every man that asketh you a reason of the hope that is in you with meekness and fear" (I Peter 3:15).

Dr. George T. Truett once related the story of a cemetery superintendent who lived in a small cottage just inside the cemetery. From his home the superintendent could watch funeral processions every day, often several a day. Finally someone asked him, "Doesn't this daily scene of sadness get on your nerves and interfere with your sleep?"

"Oh, no," he replied. "When I first began to work here I often had difficulty in sleeping, and when I did go to sleep, it was fitful and restless. I seemed to see the endless processions and the caskets of all lengths. Now I have become so hardened to these things that I could really lie down and go to sleep among the tombstones, and sleep soundly, too!"

Unlike this cemetery superintendent, the Apostle Paul never became accustomed to men dying in their sins without a Saviour. And he never lost his love for their souls.

## PAUL'S WITNESS AT JERUSALEM
### (Acts 21:10—22:24; 23:1-10)

Paul incessantly declared the gospel because he believed it to be *life* (Philippians 2:16), *light* (Psalm 119:105), and *power* (Romans 1:16).

Paul's every action, message, epistle and plan indicated that he would never get used to the fact that men are lost. He saw the great masses of humanity in Asia Minor, Palestine, and Europe as men and women without Christ. To the very end of his ministry he viewed himself as their debtor.

This is why Paul preached wherever he could. This is why he incessantly walked the highways, trod the dusty roadways, and hiked up the mountain roads, some of which were extremely narrow and precipitous. This is why he was willing to become as a Jew to the Jews without sacrificing principles of the faith.

Paul had returned from his third tour of the churches in Judea, Asia Minor, and Europe. His team included Luke, Aristarchus, and perhaps Trophimus. It was A.D. 58, and Nero was the Roman emperor. Felix was the Roman procurator, whose residence was the imperial palace at Caesarea.

This was evidently in the spring, for all along the way Paul had planned to be in Jerusalem by Pentecost.

"And when we were come to Jerusalem, the brethren received us gladly" (Acts 21:17), Luke reports. We do not know all that transpired in that warm welcome Paul and his co-workers received. But we do know that the day after Paul's arrival, James and the elders of the church in Jerusalem met with him, and Paul joyfully rehearsed all that God had done through him on behalf of the Gentiles. He must have cited the victories, listed the churches, and named some of the more prominent men and women saved at Ephesus and elsewhere. "And when they heard it, they glorified the Lord" (Acts 21:20).

But even as happy as the Jerusalem believers were to hear Paul's good news, it is apparent that the meeting of James, the Jerusalem elders, and Paul was called for a purpose other than the recounting of Paul's journey. Paul would gladly have discussed the onward progress of the gospel of the Lord Jesus as well as the opportunities for the churches of his generation and the next. But apparently these things were not on the agenda. The topics for discussion were legalistic Christianity and Paul's reputation among the Jews—both saved and unsaved.

The elders meant to protect Paul from difficulty while he was in Jerusalem. They did not want an incident to take place that could hurt the cause of the gospel. Therefore, they were bold to inform Paul of the widespread rumors. It was being said—falsely—that Paul taught Jews to apostatize from Moses and the Law and that they shouldn't have their children circumcised or walk in their Jewish customs (Acts 21:21).

Paul had never taught this. He had studiously planned not to be an offense to the Jews in any way, and yet, at the same time, to be true to Jesus Christ and his calling to preach the gospel to them.

Rumors can be cruel, very cruel! No Christian should be involved in spreading rumor for fact. But some of God's children thrive on spreading stories. They get a kind of psychological lift out of the opportunity to pass on a tale or a rumor about another brother or sister in the Lord, a family in the church or the pastor. The truth of the matter is that an addiction to spreading rumors grows out of a psychological or personality deficiency. As a child who feels insecure will misbehave, so an adult who feels insecure will pass on gossip and

Instead of indulging in gossip and idle

rumors, we are to put on love (Colossians 3:14); follow after love (I Corinthians 14:1); abound in love (II Corinthians 8:7; Philippians 1:9); continue in love (I Timothy 2:15; Hebrews 13:1); and provoke each other to love (II Corinthians 9:2; Hebrews 10:24).

It was customary for men of wealth to pay for the sacrifices required by their poorer friends.

idle rumors. Strangely enough, many times those you least expect to do this kind of thing become involved, either in spreading the rumor or in accepting it as fact.

The elders and leaders in the church at Jerusalem did not believe the rumors about Paul, but they certainly indicated that others did. So they devised a plan to put Paul in a favorable light with the Jews (verses 22,23a).

Four men had taken a vow; and the time had come to offer the usual sacrifices involved in vow-taking. Paul was to purify himself with them in the temple, and also offer sacrifices. There is every possibility that the four men did not have the money to pay for the sacrifices and thus complete their religious vows before God. So, Paul was to assume their debt and pay for all four (verses 23b-24). The Jews would see this, and the rumors would be discredited.

How did Paul view this plan? He saw no principle violated. It was not a compromise with evil; it was the suggestion of godly men whom he trusted. And, because Paul's heart was brimful of love for his Jewish brethren in Christ, he agreed to the plan (verse 26).

But the plan backfired! A riot broke out and the Jews dragged Paul out of the temple, intending to beat him to death (verses 27-30). But the Roman guard arrived, arrested Paul, and took him to the Fortress Antonia which overlooked the temple court (verses 31-36). With the permission of the captain of the guard, Paul spoke in the Hebrew tongue to the maddened crowd (verses 37-40). He witnessed of Christ, his own conversion and his calling. But at the mention of the Gentiles, the crowd grew so enraged that the chief captain,

Claudius Lysias, ordered Paul brought into the fortress and prepared to examine him by scourging (Acts 22:1-24). At this Paul asked, "Is it lawful for you to scourge a man that is a Roman, and uncondemned?" (verse 25). The captain, unaware of the precise charges against Paul, became frightened, for he knew how definite the Roman law was that a Roman citizen could not be tortured by scourging. So, he decided that Paul should appear before the Jewish high court (verses 26-30).

Acts 23:26

## PAUL'S WITNESS AT CAESAREA (Acts 24:1-27; 25:1-11; 26:1-32)

Paul appeared briefly before the Sanhedrin, but such dissension arose that he was escorted by Roman soldiers to Caesarea to stand before Felix, the Roman procurator at that time (A.D. 52-60). Paul's accusers from Jerusalem, present at this high court, made the following charge: "For we have found this man a pestilent fellow, and a mover of sedition among all the Jews throughout the world, and a ringleader of the sect of the Nazarenes: Who also hath gone about to profane the temple: whom we took, and would have judged according to our law" (Acts 24:5,6). This was the charge, for which Paul would have to stand trial before the Jews, Felix, Festus, Agrippa, and ultimately Nero.

Acts 23:1-10

While in Caesarea Paul was able to witness to Felix at least three times. First he stood before him in a public court. He later appeared before Felix twice in private. But Felix refused Christ, desiring "a convenient season" to trust in Him as Saviour (verse 25).

For further information, consult these Accent books: *Paul: Apostle of Steel and Velvet* by James T. Dyet and *Ludwig's Handbook of New Testament Rulers & Cities* by Charles Ludwig.

After two years of imprisonment, Paul stood before Porcius Festus, the new Roman procurator (A.D. 60-62). Again the Jews from Jerusalem made their accusations, and when Festus was about to use Paul politically for his own gain, Paul appealed to Caesar (Acts 25:10). This was final. Now Paul would be sent to Rome. Later, just before being taken to Rome, Paul stood before the visiting King Agrippa. Although Paul was in bonds, he witnessed of his early life and his pre-Christian activities including his religious zeal as a former Pharisee. Then he joyfully told how God had saved him on the road to Damascus. He also cited his commission from Heaven to preach. Paul's testimony was so moving that Agrippa sincerely admitted, "Almost thou persuadest me to be a Christian" (Acts 26:28). But almost is to be lost! For both Felix and Agrippa time ran out, for "now is the accepted time; behold, now is the day of salvation" (II Corinthians 6:2).

## FOOD FOR THOUGHT

*"If we are to wait to do a work for the Lord until every possible hindrance has been removed and every obstacle overcome, we will never attempt to do anything."*
—Pearls from Many Seas

## NOW TEST YOUR KNOWLEDGE

*Answer the following:*

1. Are you aware of the Biblical teaching that by nature all men are sinners and therefore lost without the Saviour?

2. After reading over such passages as Matthew 28:18-20, Mark 16:15, Acts 1:8, do you sense any personal responsibility to witness for Christ?

3. Have you made it a habit to witness for Christ at least once a day?

4. Which is better—to make it a habit to distribute as many tracts and speak to as many people as possible during the day, or to ask the Lord at the beginning of each day to lead you specifically to the person or persons to whom He would have you witness?

5. When the Spirit of God leads you to the person He has chosen for you to witness to, do you know unmistakably that this is the person?

6. Is soul winning confined to those cases where someone actually leads the soul to Christ?

7. Have you ever had a part in winning a soul to Christ?

# THE UNFINISHED TASK

ACTS 27; 28

## EVERY DAY WITH THE WORD

| | | |
|---|---|---|
| Monday | Winning souls | Proverbs 11 |
| Tuesday | Light for the Gentiles | Isaiah 60 |
| Wednesday | Shining stars | Daniel 12 |
| Thursday | Pray and work | Nehemiah 4:1-6 |
| Friday | Prepared to preach | Ezra 7:1-10 |
| Saturday | What to preach | Psalm 19 |
| Sunday | Where to preach | Acts 1:1-8 |

Several years ago some wealthy residents of Richmond, Virginia, were asked to sign a petition against a small church. The petition, which was to be presented to the city council, claimed that the congregation's singing was disturbing. When the document was brought to a Jewish resident of the community for his signature, he pushed it away, explaining, "I cannot sign this. If I believed as they do that my Messiah had come, I would shout it from the housetops and on every street in Richmond, and nobody could stop me!"

This is precisely what the early church did. They believed that Messiah had come, so in fulfillment of the Great Commission they went forth to tell the world. First, the Jews, then the Samaritans, finally the Gentiles—all were told of God's provision for sin in the person of the Messiah and Saviour, Jesus Christ.

But the message did not go out without consequence to those who spread it. Many lost their lives, others had their reputations ruined, still others were repeatedly beaten and otherwise persecuted for the sake of the gospel. Yet they were faithful to their Saviour, to the Word, and to their fellow believers.

## THE WITNESS EN ROUTE TO ROME
(Acts 27:1—28:16)

The dock at Caesarea bustled with activity. A huge merchant ship was being readied for departure. Scores of people milled around, loading the vessel, bidding loved ones good-bye, or just curiously observing the goings-on. Among the passengers was a man who, although he probably had no family to see him off, was surrounded by concerned friends. The Apostle Paul was being transported to Rome, and many Christians were there to bid him good-bye and to assure him of their continued prayers for his safety and well-being.

Why was this man traveling the great distance to the capital city of the Roman Empire? Was he taking a long-needed and well-deserved vacation? Was he going to start another church? Was he delivering gifts to Roman believers? No—the Apostle Paul was making this extended journey for one purpose—to appear before Nero, the emperor, to present his defense of his Christian life. He was guilty of no crime, yet his appeal to Caesar made it mandatory for him to stand before the emperor (Acts 26:32). Finally the ship was ready to set sail, and the saddened crowd slowly disbanded. Paul was on his way to Rome.

God's message of salvation is for everyone—regardless of race, religion, economic status, or family background. God sent His Son for every man, woman, and child that has ever lived or will ever live (John 3:16).

The early Christians were extremely loyal to one another. Whenever one of them had a problem or a need, the others were ready and willing to help. Perhaps our churches should take a lesson from these first-century believers.

There are other centurions mentioned in Scripture. See Matthew 8:5-13; Luke 7:2-10; Acts 10; 11.

See Acts 27:2. Adramyttium, on the Aegean sea-coast, was a shipbuilding center. Evidently Paul's vessel had been built at this port, or it was owned by someone there.

There were 276 people on board the ship (Acts 27:37).

On this journey, Paul was in the custody of the centurion, Julius. This man, a military expert who was in charge of 100 Roman soldiers, was courteous and genuinely concerned for those in his charge. This doesn't mean he was weak and vulnerable to any who played upon his sympathy. Not at all; the very fact that he was a centurion indicates that he was brave and fully reliable, for Rome commissioned only highly courageous and trustworthy men to the rank of centurion. Some centurions were known to be cruel, not caring how much pain and suffering they caused others. But Julius was different. He even allowed Paul to visit some friends while the ship docked at Sidon the day after the travelers left Caesarea (Acts 27:3).

When the boat left Sidon, the captain steered it to go south of Cyprus, for "the winds were contrary" (verse 4). It was not the season for sailing in the Mediterranean, for between the months of October and March the winds were far too fierce for even the biggest ships and the most able-bodied seamen. Why the ship was sailing during these hazardous winter months, we do not know. But apparently the Roman government felt the need was urgent enough to risk the lives of many soldiers and other passengers.

When the ship reached the port of Myra at Lycia, the centurion put the prisoners on another ship that was headed to Rome (verses 5,6). This was a common practice in those days, for Myra was a busy port and larger ships often came there, picking up additional cargo and passengers on their journeys from Alexandria to Rome.

As they sailed opposite Cnidus they moved southward, hoping to sail below Crete. They passed Salmone and The Fair Havens, hoping to put up for the winter at Phenice (Phoenix) at the end of the cape.

However, at this point they encountered winds of hurricane velocity (Euroclydons, vicious northeast winds that blew down from the mountains of Crete). They could not advance in the face of these winds so, lowering the sails, they allowed the ship to be driven at will by the winds. For fourteen days they despaired of getting the ship under control.

Were the events of this account all there was to Paul's long journey, that in itself would be exciting enough. But not only did Paul encounter and endure the danger of a boisterous sea, but he also gained spiritual victories while on board that musty ship.

Paul knew God, and God had given him a word for the passengers. God came to him in the night, exhorting, "Fear not, Paul . . . God hath given thee all them that sail with thee" (Acts 27:24). Paul was optimistic, for he believed God. So he witnessed to the passengers, declaring that "I believe God, that it shall be even as it was told me" (verse 25).

This could not help but impress Julius, the soldiers and the seamen. They were men of great courage, yet the angry sea was more than they could normally endure.

After fourteen days, the sailors, thinking they were nearing land, attempted to abandon ship and its precious cargo of souls in order to avoid being killed in the wreck that seemed inevitable (verses 27-29). But Paul discovered the midnight plan and reported it to the soldiers, pointing out that their lives depended upon the sailors remain-

There are times when even the world likes to have a Christian around. Keep this in mind and take an interest in the needs and problems of people. A little encouragement goes a long way with most people.

ing on board ship. The soldiers cut the ropes of the lifeboat, allowing it to drop into the sea, thus removing the sailors' chance to escape (verses 30-32).

The next day the sailors ran the ship aground and all passengers made it safely to the shore of what proved to be Melita (the island of Malta) (verses 40-44).

How would it have been had you been in Paul's place? Do you inspire trust in God on the part of others? Do others feel safe when they watch you in times of need, in times of perplexity, when the contrary winds blow? Are you, by your example, showing others that this is the way they must trust God when they face contrary winds in the future? Or do you always expect the worst, not putting your trust in Him?

A certain man related this personal experience: "I once saw a sign saying, 'Cheer up—things could be worse!' So, I cheered up, and sure enough, things got worse." Perhaps you say, "I will trust God. I will not be a poor testimony to my family, to those with whom I work, to my friends in the church." And then, even with your resolve, things seem to get worse and the winds blow more fiercely. Keep trusting God—He knows what is ahead and He is in complete control.

Romans 8:28

Paul was not only a trusting Christian, but he was a humble man, a man who believed he ought to work as well as pray. He was not too big to do the work required in a given situation. Indeed, he prayed, but he also helped throw excess things overboard to lighten the ship. He carried wood for a fire to warm the passengers after the ship ran aground. And he healed the sick and dying at Melita. Yes, Paul's witness was verbal, but it was

Acts 27:38; 28:3

also intensely practical.

Acts 28:8,9

After three months on Melita, the shipwrecked group proceeded by ship to Syracuse and then on to Rhegium and the port of Puteoli on the Italian mainland. From there they traveled overland to the imperial city. At last Paul stood in the city of the Caesars and beheld something of the vastness, the greatness of Rome (Acts 28:1-16).

## THE WITNESS IN ROME
## (Acts 28:17-31)

After arriving in Rome, Paul was permitted to live in his own hired (rented) quarters (Acts 28:30). And he didn't worry about where he would get the money to pay the rent. Paul was the kind of man who believed that if God could control a storm, He could also control daily circumstances and supply daily needs.

While Paul was living in Rome, he was able to have as many visitors as he wanted, since he lived in his own home. True, he did have a guard, but he was allowed a great amount of freedom. His Christian friends could come, and many did. He also invited unsaved Jews to come and reason with him concerning Jesus. And some of these Jews put their trust in the Messiah.

If something has restricted your ministry physically, remember that many believers have turned their handicaps into pulpits from which to declare God's truth.

Paul's ministry in Rome was not only a spoken ministry. From his hired house he sent letters to the Ephesians, the Colossians, the Philippians, and to Philemon. Faithful men of God carried them to their destination. And Paul's written ministry, that took place over 1900 years ago, will never die!

I Peter 1:25

Paul was released from Rome in A.D. 63 after standing trial before Nero. However, in A.D. 64

Rome burned, and great persecutions broke out against Christians. Being a Christian was considered a capital offense. Therefore some believe that in the midst of the persecution Paul fled Rome and went to Macedonia, then to Asia Minor, Spain, back to Asia Minor, Macedonia, Ephesus, and finally Nicopolis, where he was arrested again in A.D. 68. He was taken to Rome, tried, and put to death in A.D. 68.

Throughout the centuries since Paul, untold millions have died without Christ. Today countless villages are without a gospel witness, and hundreds of languages and dialects are yet to receive their own translation of the Scriptures. We still face the unfinished task of touching the untouched and reaching the unreached millions with the gospel.

In our hands rests a glorious heritage. We have been given a heritage of truth, evangelism, and courage. Christians must awaken to the sound of millions of feet marching every day—marching into a vast eternity without hope. What God intends for us to do on behalf of souls must be done now, for tomorrow may be too late. Nothing lies so near to the heart of God as winning the lost. This is the business of the church; we dare not neglect it.

> Stir me, oh! stir me, Lord, I care not how,
> But stir my heart in passion for the world!
> Stir me to give, to go—but most to pray:
>
> Stir, till the blood-red banner be unfurled
> O'er lands that still in deepest darkness lie,
> O'er deserts where no cross is lifted high.

You cannot by any means reach all of these people, but you can do your part. Are you faithful in giving to missions? How's your prayer life when it comes to interceding for missionaries and other Christian workers? Do you seek to win the lost in your own community? If everyone does his part, more people will be reached with the saving message of the gospel.

*Stir me, oh! stir me, Lord. Thy heart was*
  *stirred*
*By love's intensest fire, till Thou didst*
  *give*
*Thine only Son, Thy best beloved One,*
*Even to the dreadful cross, that I might*
  *live;*
*Stir me to give myself so back to Thee*
*That Thou canst give Thyself again*
  *through me.*

—Author unknown

## FOOD FOR THOUGHT

*"The supply of God's grace is suitable for our need, sufficient in its bestowment, sustaining in its blessing, and adapted to our requirements."*

—F. E. Marsh

*Underline the correct answers:*

1. The ship that Paul boarded was a ship of: (Adramyttium; Corinth; Alexandria).

2. Humanly speaking, it appeared as though the ship would: (reach harbor safely; weather the storm; perish).

3. The occupants of the ship finally landed on the island of: (Melita; Crete; Cyprus).

4. In Rome Paul lived: (in Luke's home; in the dungeon; in his own hired quarters).

5. When a shipwreck seemed inevitable, Paul: (hid in the lower deck; prayed and encouraged others; panicked).

6. Paul healed: (Silas' brother; Julius' mother; Publius' father).

7. When Paul arrived in Rome he: (called the Jews together; organized a church; smuggled Bibles to the believers).

8. (Justus; Publius; Julius) was responsible for Paul during the journey.

## RECOMMENDED BOOKS FOR FURTHER STUDY

You may wish to do further study in the book of Acts. If so, any of the following volumes would be an excellent choice to aid you in your study. Consult your local Christian bookstore or your church library.

A DEVOTIONAL COMMENTARY ON THE ACTS OF THE APOSTLES by J. C. Macaulay, Eerdmans Publishing Co., Grand Rapids (1946). A delightful devotional commentary.

ACTS OF THE APOSTLES by A. C. Gaebelein, Loizeaux Brothers, Neptune, New Jersey (1961). A thorough, quite readable volume for the Bible student.

ARCHAEOLOGY AND THE NEW TESTAMENT by Merrill F. Unger, Zondervan Publishing House, Grand Rapids (1962). Chapters 7-18 are especially helpful in a study of the book of Acts.

BARNES ON THE NEW TESTAMENT, Baker Book House, Grand Rapids (1961). A fine general commentary for the layman.

COMMENTARY ON HOLY SCRIPTURE (ACTS) by John Peter Lange, Zondervan Publishing House, Grand Rapids. A commentary for the advanced student.

LECTURES ON ACTS by H. A. Ironside, Loizeaux Brothers, Neptune, New Jersey (1943). A great commentary for the average Christian, supplying extremely practical material.

**PAUL: APOSTLE OF STEEL AND VELVET** by James T. Dyet, Accent Books, Denver (1976). An inspiring portrayal of the apostle, whose life and ministry span more than half the book of Acts.

**THE ACTS OF THE APOSTLES** by Charles Caldwell Ryrie, Moody Press, Chicago (1961). A splendid addition to any library.

**THE ACTS OF THE APOSTLES** by F. F. Bruce, Zondervan Publishing House, Grand Rapids. An in-depth commentary for the one who wishes to have deeper knowledge of the book of Acts.

**UNGER'S BIBLE DICTIONARY** by Merrill F. Unger, Moody Press, Chicago (1960). This has become one of the standard Bible dictionaries for use by all Bible believers.